SACRED SITES AND PLACES OF POWER 3

THE SCOTTISH STONE CIRCLE ORACLE CARDS HANDBOOK

HEATHER CHARNLEY

Copyright © 2017 Heather Charnley

© Purple Spirit Press 2017

All rights reserved. No part of this publication may be reproduced, stored in a retrieval system, or transmitted in any form or by any means, electronic, mechanical, photocopying, recording or otherwise without the prior permission of the copyright owner.

Using original art work
and writing by
Heather Charnley

ISBN 978-1-907042-35-5

Dedicated to Olivia Robertson
Co-Founder of Fellowship of Isis, Ireland
for introducing me to the goddess energy,
and Kathleen Murray who had worked energetically
on the Aberdeen stones and introduced me to them

PURPLE SPIRIT PRESS
Heather Charnley

Email: purplespiritpress@gmail.com
heathercharnley@googlmail.com
www.heathercharnleyspiritualart.co.uk

SACRED SITES AND PLACES OF POWER 3
THE SCOTTISH STONE CIRCLE ORACLE CARDS

INDEX

The foreword	4
How to use the cards	5
Plan views of stones' placements in circle	7
Chapter 1 – the twelve apostles' stone circle	8
Insights of the twelve apostles' stone circle	24
Chapter 2 – the mother circle	29
Insights of the mother circle	38
Chapter 3 – the Loanhead of Daviot stone circle	47
Insights of the Loanhead of Daviot stone circle	58
Chapter 4 – the Easter Arquoithies stone circle	63
Insights of the Easter Arquoithies stone circle	75
Chapter 5 – the Sunhoney stone circle	81
Insights of the Sunhoney stone circle	93
Resumé of insights for quick reference	100
Heather's work philosophy	104
Contact details	105

SACRED SITES & PLACES OF POWER 3
THE SCOTTISH STONE CIRCLE ORACLE CARDS

FOREWORD BY HEATHER CHARNLEY

This is the third in the Sacred Sites and Places of Power series. Over the years I have been inspired to travel all over the country, and the first book took me far and wide, including America, and the book covered many places over Britain and America. The second book was locally based in Northumberland, and so it was a book that I felt inspired to go into one region more in depth. As there was little history available, I used my intuition to create a story, which simply came through me, and I strongly felt it was relative to some past events involving local wise women.

In this third one of the series, having used my intuition within the second book, I took it further to create the oracle cards set, based on five stone circles I visited, three of them in 2005 when I visited Kathleen Murray near Aberdeen, and the other circles later.

The card pack is available to buy on my website

A few years ago I did a priestess course with the FOI, and during that I was meditating on a stone circle of choice, and began to write information about one of the stone circles visited within that time, which is the Mother Circle, and then I knew shortly after that the oracle card set was born!

Within the Oracle Card set, there are the five card packs, one per stone circle, with information about each stone within the sets, an image of each stone circle, directions of how to get to each site, and instructions on how to use the cards. They differ from many card packs, because of the energetic vibrations from the cards themselves, holding them to the third eye to receive insight and healing, and I am not aware of other packs that have that capacity.

SACRED SITES & PLACES OF POWER 3

THE SCOTTISH STONE CIRCLE ORACLE CARDS

There are 5 sets that comprise this oracle card set, based on 5 stone circles in Scotland. Each stone circle set links to the 5 elements, and the individual cards per stone have their own qualities. The characteristics of each stone are given in each set's information.

THE FIVE SETS:
TWELVE APOSTLES STONE CIRCLE: - AIR. The card sets each have their own characteristics, for the Twelve Apostles Stone Circle is more of a knowledge-based set.

THE MOTHER CIRCLE: - WATER. The Mother Circle is very intuitive, of a seer ship nature, and gives the story of a seer, Ailspaeth, who lived and worked there.

LOANHEAD OF DAVIOT CIRCLE: - EARTH. Yet again, the Loanhead of Daviot Circle links to the subtle realms well. The words I received here were 'it is a gateway to other worlds, to help with soul retrieval work'.

EASTER ARQUOITHIES STONE CIRCLE: - FIRE. At the Easter Arquoithies site, I found the energy here is definitely fiery. Not physical, but spiritual fire, where energy moves and stimulates. It rises from the Earth and can bring succour to many. To sum up, I found this site good as a place to ask questions, receive divine answers and gather inspiration.

SUNHONEY STONE CIRCLE: - ETHER. At the Sunhoney Circle, this pack deals with the final release of individual or personal karmic connections, so that the individual can focus on higher frequencies that are available via this site. It also links in higher frequency energy into the Earth, and can be directed where required.

HOW TO USE THE CARDS:

The method is to spread the set around you as if you were inside the given stone circle you are working with.

Enter into meditation with the cards, intuiting which card wishes to give you some kind of message or wisdom, and work with it. I often begin with going around all the cards in the set, and then in the next session, see if individual cards have additional messages to add. On average I usually have between three and eight sessions, however, there is no limit!

I always take a notebook into the session with me and jot information down as it comes to me, other people may prefer to do this afterwards. As it is an experiential activity, you may find your own methods of working with them.

I have recorded all that I have experienced, and salient points have been added into the text, included with them are various questions that I asked, and they may be useful to begin with, for anyone who uses the cards, no doubt the user will ask their own questions in due course. I shall also add a photograph of each site with directions to find the five stone circles.

PLAN VIEWS OF STONE'S PLACEMENTS

12 Apostles Stone Circle

1. God's Altar Stone
2. Governor Stone
3. Harmoniser Stone
4. Evening Star Stone
5. Gatekeeper Stone
6. Storekeeper Stone
7. Watch Stone
8. Grail Cup Stone
9. Knowledge Stone
10. Kind Stone
11. Druid Stone
12. Thunder Stone
13. Outlier Stone

The Mother Stone Circle

1. Mother Stone
2. Seer Stone
3. Prophecy Stone
4. Ring Stone
5. Fairy Stones
6. The Guides
7. Sacred Stones
8. Altar Stone

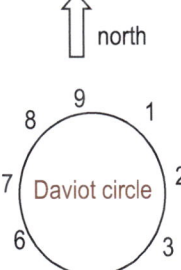

Daviot Stone Circle

1. Teaching Stone
2. Praying Stone
3. Guider Stone
4. Altar Reflector Stone
5. Dreamer Stone
6. Adoration Stone
7. Mistletoe Stone
8. Ringleader Stone
9. Altar Stones

Easter Arquoithies Stone Circle

1. Scryer Stone
2. Inspirer Stone
3. Wisdom Stone
4. Initiation Stone
5. Saintly Stone
6. Grounding Stone
7. Effulgence Stone
8. Sage Stone
9. Searcher Stone
10. Altar Stones

Sunhoney Stone Circle

1. Initiation of Secrets Stone
2. Thought Edifier Stone
3. Emotional Release Stone
4. Tender Stone
5. Garland Stone
6. Warrior Stone
7. Opening of 3rd Eye Stone
8. Sword in the Stone
9. Releasing Stone
10. Altar Stones

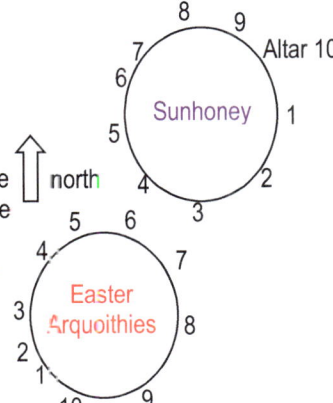

SACRED SITES & PLACES OF POWER 3
THE SCOTTISH STONE CIRCLE ORACLE CARDS

SACRED SITES & PLACES OF POWER
THE SCOTTISH ORACLE CARDS
Element - Air

THE TWELVE APOSTLES STONE CIRCLE

This stone circle lies to the north side of Dumfries, along the A76 to Kilmarnock. Dumfries is reached via the A75, to the west of Carlisle and Gretna, to the west of the M74. The stone circle is situated near Holywood Village, although not sign posted, take a left turn up a minor road if coming from the south from Dumfries, just before reaching Holywood. The stone circle is on flat ground, just a quarter of a mile along there, where there will be another left turn beside the outlier, as shown in this image below.

12 apostles stone circle with outlier

TWELVE APOSTLES STONE CIRCLE

1. God's Altar Stone

'My energy rises and falls simultaneously because I am linked to both Heaven and Earth. I am a stabilising influence here, and energies brought here I distribute and give out into the circle, and to those people who come, and that included the priesthood of old. I also give out to all creatures who live in the area, both above and below ground.'

To see the energy, it is simply a shaft of white light that encompasses the stone through which energy travels upwards and downwards, and streams of concentrated energy lift up out of the top of the squat stone, which rises to the apex of the circle. From this, a shaft of light that overlights the planet, or to be precise, it appears like a disc of light over the circle because the vibrant energy only picks out that part of the layer, and it is really a huge auric-like layer around the planet.

The priest or priestess would stand here in order to bring in inspiration to invoke the care of neophytes and then ask them to stand by this stone while they did whatever instructions or work during their initial learning periods.

Another significance of this stone is that it is placed, not only beside the Governor Stone, which brings in energy from the outlier, but on its other side is the Thunder Stone, which also brings in energy powerfully. No wonder this is the God's Altar Stone!

This stone is on the northern side predominantly, and in considering the ancient Celtic ceremonial circle layout, the northern place is of wisdom, and of the Earth, and therefore in the stillness of this element much can be contemplated on.

TWELVE APOSTLES STONE CIRCLE

2. The Governor Stone

'Earth-centred energy comes from the outlier into me, and from there I distribute it around the circle, and I determine how much is required at any given time. I am the 'anti-surge suppressor' to ensure the energies brought in are uniform. The priests and priestesses of old knew about this stone's characteristic, the relevant energies of each of the stones, and the purposes behind making these circles. They could touch the lives of our ancestors, the Neoliths, with this knowledge, and so they understood about electricity long before the Industrial Age!'

This stone also works closely with the Thunder Stone, which is situated on the other side of the God's Altar Stone.

'Every circle has a Governor Stone that accepts and regulates external energy coming in, but it may not be called a Governor Stone, and for instance, the one at Easter Arquoithies is called The Grounding Stone. Some powerful stones in circles act as both a Governor Stone and an outlier, In this case, like some others, the energy is transmitted from the outlier, and then it can come straight into the circle via myself, the Governor Stone.'

The energy seen here coming into the energy of the stone is of the descending arc of light coming into the exterior side of the Governor Stone, slightly west of due north, and therefore is NNW. The energy over the stone is like a dome of gently amassing residual power, and represents the actual energy stored from the outlier awaiting distribution around the circle, wanting to always keep a supply that can be fed around as and when on a constant basis.

The shape of that store of energy is like a spherical dome, with gently rising currents of energy within it, and with an arched and broadened flame-like shape above it. The energy is fairly quiescent because much of it is being stored and regulated, but the sensation below the stone is that of energy in motion, which is distributed at ground level and slightly below as well.

This stone is on the northern side, and more due north than the God's Altar Stone. In considering the ancient Celtic ceremonial circle layout, the northern place is of wisdom, and of the Earth, and therefore in the stillness of this element much can be contemplated on.

TWELVE APOSTLES STONE CIRCLE

3. The Harmoniser Stone

At the Harmoniser Stone much energy has been coming via the God's Altar Stone from that storehouse of energy above, and also from both the Governor Stone and the outlier, and previous to all that, the energy from the Thunder Stone that brings in energy from the heavens and the Earth. Although the Governor Stone is the anti-surge suppressor in the circle, the Harmoniser Stone takes the energy offered after the Governor Stone has assimilated it all, and synthesises it so that it is ready and available in the right way, not just for the circle, but for each individual stone.

The energy of the Harmoniser is simply a big flame of light above it, as the energy emanates as a result of this incoming energy from the outlier and other stones. It radiates from the top of the stone and overlaps its shoulders, and has three other smaller flames inside it. Below the large flame, all around the stone, there are lots of smaller flames glowing brightly. The main colour here is white with golden edges, and the whole configuration is surrounded by an aura of golden light. This fiery energy of the stone transmutes and changes the given energy very easily as a result, and makes sure it is pure enough for the stones, and the circle as a whole.

In the ancient Celtic ceremonial circle layout, there are the four quarters or directions, plus north east and south east. At the north is the place of the Hidden One, and of wisdom. It is also a stone for insight and so it brings that wisdom of the northern direction. The other stones previously mentioned are contributing towards doing this, and the Harmoniser is the culmination of wisdom gleaned from this northern direction.

TWELVE APOSTLES STONE CIRCLE

4. The Evening Star Stone

This stone is placed at the north east, and links to the scryer's position, as given in the traditional layout of the Celtic circle as given in ceremonial use. Here, it is also an alignment place, forming a link with the stars to bring that heavenly energy from above, that stellar light, into the circle. One star in question from which the alignment takes place is Capella. It is not that there is anything on the stone that deliberately shows alignment in a physical manner to the star like a telescope, it is more that the stone has been psychically attuned in order to link spiritually to Capella.

Many stones at circles were said to have been linked to Capella, and what does Capella have to say to us? Capella was one of several sighting stones, especially useful as it was a fixed star, not given to orbiting as such, and Capella marks the month of February at the position of north north-east. The other stars of note for the yearly calendar are Antares that was linked to May, and Arcturus that was linked to August.

This stone is nearest to the Scryer in the ancient Celtic ceremonial circle, and the right hand pillar or Pendragon in the modern Celtic circle. It also links to mid-summer sunrise, as due east and south east link to equinoxes and mid-summer sunrise respectively.

There is a notch or hollowed area on the northern side of the stone, with a flame-like energy over it, and this is the aligning place, for on looking up from there, the star is seen. The energy shown above is a mass of flames that rise to a point at the apex with that smaller flame inside that hovers over that notch.

Having a fixed location meant a lot for the ancients, for it was a mainstay for calculations, and like the nature of spiritual subjects, the supernal requirements for all manner of things to sustain life is constant, and therefore the ancient ones who calculated and made this circle, and the many others, held great affection for this star.

This stone and the next two, the Gatekeeper Stone and the Storekeeper Stone all link to the north east and eastern side. The north east point is the first arm of the Awen, which is situated at the eastern side of a Celtic ceremonial circle, and is the triple rays of supernal light that the eastern side holds, and this stone, the Evening Star Stone is placed there.

TWELVE APOSTLES STONE CIRCLE

5. The Gatekeeper Stone

This is a meditation stone and I was invited to sit on it, and I felt very much at home there. It can link to past lives, and also to aspects of nature, linking to trees, Earth energies and spirits in the locality. The stone has a gentle and kind energy. Looking at its energy I saw it like a white fountain coming up out of the centre of it, which cascades over and around the stone, enveloping it in a lovely peaceful cocoon-like atmosphere. This gentle energy feels safe, and so it is conducive to dealing with past life issues, and the fact you are invited to sit there, makes it idea and inviting. I have tried the stone and it does help with past life issues.

The stone is next to the Scryer Stone, so it also resonates to that 'scryer' place in the Celtic circle layout, and can lend itself to bringing in such insights, for the energy is bright and still.

It is the middle stone of the trio at the eastern side, the others being the Evening Star Stone and the Storekeeper Stone. As this stone's name suggests, it is a gatekeeper because it is a place where 'mysteries' or information that needs to be revealed with care and therefore guidance from the spirits here, may be required.

A gatekeeper was also a knowledgeable person who would preside over and initate the teaching of insights to a candidate, to bring in greater wisdom with care, and would know just how much a person would be able to deal with at any given occasion.

This stone was the companion of neophytes, as they went to regularly purify themselves.

This stone shares some of the energy at the north east with the Evening Star Stone, and is the second arm of the Druidic Awen, which has the three arms at the eastern side of the Celtic ceremonial circle.

TWELVE APOSTLES STONE CIRCLE

6. The Storekeeper Stone

This is a big strong stone, which is linked with the Earth, and is constantly bringing up big bold spiralling energies up a wide shaft of white light that is almost as wide as the stone itself.

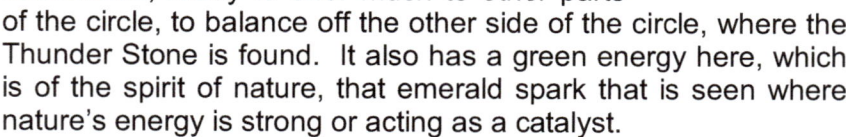

Therefore this strong energy is like a storehouse, ready to offer much to other parts of the circle, to balance off the other side of the circle, where the Thunder Stone is found. It also has a green energy here, which is of the spirit of nature, that emerald spark that is seen where nature's energy is strong or acting as a catalyst.

The phrase 'lights the fires of the mind' also came to me when I visited the stones, and suggests that the green spark of energy as well as the Earth's spirals provide energy to be a catalyst of insights for all life, including humans.

This is the third of the trio of eastern stones, and the Storekeeper's name hints of the storehouse of energy this stone is capable of handling on a constant basis. Unlike the Evening Star Stone, both the Gatekeeper and this Storekeeper Stone both bring up energy from the Earth, linking the earth to air, and bringing a grounding capacity to it, so that insights will be much more practical and immediate.

Although this stone is due east, and is a powerful stone, the Druids would have called this the Elevated Chair, but actually may have used the next stone along, the Watch Stone, as it has certain distinctive capacities relevant to the Elevated Chair. This stone is really the third arm of the Celtic Awen even though it shares the due east with the Gate Keeper and the energetic value of the Watch Stone.

All this focus on the eastern side denotes this circle's emphasis on the element of air.

TWELVE APOSTLES STONE CIRCLE

7. The Watch Stone

This is called the Watch Stone because it has guardian-like capabilities, which is appropriate since it is on the south east side where the third arm of the Druidic Awen is traditionally situated. In the Druidic and ancient Celtic ceremonial circles, this position would be called the Guardian of the Mysteries, and the left hand pillar for modern ones. The left hand direction given here refers to the Earth-based and lunar orientation rather than solar, and certainly doesn't indicate black magic.

In this case, the high priest or priestess used this stone since it has the right capacity, and so this stone was used for the elevated chair, for one who watches or presides over his flock at ceremonies and at other times. The high priest would stand here and oversee any ceremonies, and was able, with the energy of this stone, to view individuals who came to him for help, and those in the ceremonies who aspired to be initiated in to the mysteries. He or she would be able to tell by viewing a person's aura, as to whether they were ready, and the spirit of the stone would tell the high priest much as well.

Usually the elevated chair is at due east, and so I think that the south eastern position was used in this instance as much Earthly energy was needed for this site, and was one that offered much wisdom and teaching.

The energy around the stone is like a mass of flames that rises to a point well above the stone's apex, the same height again as the stone itself, and from the apex successive flame-like images rise upwards from there to the top of the flames' energy field. This energy is the effect of the stone's capacity, for if you link to the stone it will show you a portal inside it that acts like a scrying mirror, so you can gain insights. On viewing its energies, as the energy comes from the Earth, but looks fiery and solar powered on appearance, and so it is therefore a fusion of the two energy directions to allow this Watching Stone force to be used by the high priest or priestess.

TWELVE APOSTLES STONE CIRCLE

8. The Grail Cup Stone

This stone shares the capacities of the third arm of the Awen at the south eastern position, where the Watch Stone operates, yet the stone is actually placed more to the southern area. This is because it has more of the energy of the Earth rising up from below it, in order to consolidate as a chalice with flames emanating from it. This is as a result of the strong Earth energies, and although strong, it is powerful yet gentle, and is the combination of gentleness and strength that forms a chalice with flames, as male and female energies are combined here.

The image shows the three stones with the biggest at the centre that comprise the Grail Cup Stone. The stones are surrounded by the usual standard etheric auric layer of light, and above that, a layer of flames that are white. Out of this layer, just above the central stone is the Grail Cup image with its pedestal rising from the flames, and inside the chalice of white light are more flames gently burning. Surrounding all of the flames and chalice there is an encirclement of energy that has flame-like edges, and is a pale golden yellow.

Surrounding all of the above, including the stones themselves, is another layer of energy that is more pointed at the top, and is a brilliant white colour.

This stone would be a place where priests and priestesses could derive inspiration for teaching neophytes, and they would be the ones further along the pathway, since the stone brings up stronger illumination within its feminine chalice energy, and that the stone is near the Watch Stone too, so it garners its potency. The fires also help to aid the burning away of the dross, so that illumination will be the result.

TWELVE APOSTLES STONE CIRCLE

9. The Knowledge Stone

As the stones have been approached by yourself by going southwards in a clockwise direction, the increase in fiery energy has been experienced, and now the circuit is progressing westwards, and so is moving to a less outgoing quarter. The expressive fiery energy is seen here to have been culminated as an inner knowledge and wisdom, and so therefore when reflection upon the spiritual truths begins, then the wisdom becomes known.

The western side is the place called Goronwy or the seat of the moon, where a candidate gains entry to a circle during a ceremony, and then works his or her way round clockwise. If he or she continues from the south, back to the west again, it would then be a place of true reflection, having returned in order to reflect on the whole circuit, and have more insight than when he or she began.

There is a more intellectual and left-brained air about this stone, but not excessively, as the knowledge was born of intuition. In the image, the radiance of the etheric is seen around the stone, and out of the apex there is a wide, vertical shaft of white light, which goes up to the apex, as with all the other stones' energies here. Inside this shaft a few feet up hangs an eye image that is surrounded by etheric energy, and inside it is a pupil holding two intersecting circles representing eternity. This shows that the knowledge attained is spiritual, timeless, and transcends all the Earthly knowledge, and so is a fusion of intellect and intuition.

There is a being here who calls himself the 'Lighter of the Way', and I could see him holding out a candlestick with a very bright flame. He will answer questions people can put to him that will help in any way to understand the mysteries, and help solve any problems. He can be reached by saying his name three times, and asking 'please speak to me'. By way of thanks, do some kind of service in your community somehow, he says.

TWELVE APOSTLES STONE CIRCLE

10. The Kind Stone

This stone is a very gentle one, with soft glowing energy that is very bright, with the atmosphere of mellow light shining on rose petals, and emanates a rose-tinted atmosphere of unconditional love towards those who would wish to experience it.

To look at the stone, it has the usual etheric radiance, and then is surrounded completely by an emanation of light shafts gently rising upwards, and has a pale rose colour with golden lights shimmering within it. Surrounding the whole of that light is a dome of white light that is surrounded by a halo of golden energy.

This dome of light encapsulates the loving energy that comes out of the Earth, and so, consolidates it into a temple-like place for the aspirant to visit. Even high priests can view it, and receive good effect when dealing with responsibilities of the earthly plane.

This stone and the Gatekeeper both have a similar gentle energy, the latter has a meditative air that encourages you to have good insights, and this, the Kind Stone, helps you to reflect on what you have received, or whatever else is in your mind, and takes things on further to resolution and mature reflection, hence its kindness in helping one to achieve results. In this way it heals and brings in beneficence, and a genuine love for all of life.

Many gnomes work under this stone as they do for the Gatekeeper Stone, to bring those treasureable energies to the fore. In general, they help to bring energies upwards all over the planet, and choose the appropriate places of operation. They said that they work all around the circle, but in these two places of the Kind Stone and Gatekeeper Stone, they collaborate with the elves and fairies to modify the energies there to enhance that gentleness.

TWELVE APOSTLES STONE CIRCLE

11. The Druid Stone

We are still within the western side here, that is reflective and of the wisdom found from going 'full circle', and it follows on from the Kind Stone, as showing the maturity at the west, as it takes the insights from the Gatekeeper Stone, and culminates the wisdom, as mentioned.

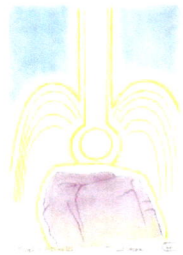

It is the Druidic Stone, for the Druids in olden times trained for many years, covering a wide amount of knowledge by the end of their tuition, and became wizards, priests, counsellors and much else, a potent person in the community. I feel that in this stone is held the potent wisdom of many Druids, ready to give counsel.

Just hovering over the top of the stone with its etheric layer shining, is a spherical shape like the sun or moon, and it is a bright sphere that shines its radiance to the onlooker who seeks to know things.

A vertical shaft of light descends down to this sphere, and into a surrounding layer of radiant light around it. Around this sphere a fountain of light emerges from either side of it and cascades down the sides of the Druid Stone and into the ground, linking to the Earth.

As said, the sphere could be either or both sun and moon, for it is a reflective place, where much contemplation brings wisdom, strength of insight and inner calm.

When the solar and lunar realms are at peace with one another and working together, for the knowledge that is solar has matured to become wisdom, and when the sun and moon come together, then greater soul integration takes place, resulting in inner peace. From that place of stillness, insights and wisdom can come much more easily.

TWELVE APOSTLES STONE CIRCLE

12. The Thunder Stone

'I am, in fact, the most powerful stone of the whole circle, for like thunder, I bring in very powerful energies, but I also link to the Governor Stone, for all the energy I bring would be too much for the circle to bear.

Much of my dynamic energy comes in surges from the heavens, or rather, that layer of light above. Some of the thunder stones have energy that comes out of the Earth, and so is also powerful, but has a different effect being that of the Goddess, and for instance, there is a very large diamond shaped stone at Avebury with that name as well, that stands at the gate to the northern avenue.

This stone is very large and supine, as if lying at an angle on its side, and it has cup shaped markings on the side facing inwards into the circle. A huge shaft of white light descends downwards, enveloping the stone, and a six-petalled flower shape can be seen underneath the stone, denoting the linking of this heavenly energy with that of the Earth, and the Earth's energy is flowering as a result.

To emphasize that, there is a spinning vortex at the centre of the flower shape, and the whole flower moves gently clockwise, spinning around.

As a result, a vast mass of energy rises upwards to meet that which descends. Like the kundalini's reaction in humans, energy comes in through the crown chakra, and filters down to the base chakra, which is activated, and in turn, stimulates the other chakras, and then the kundalini becomes activated over time, and it finally rises up to join the source of the energy that originally descended.

So it is a powerful kundalini stone. Like thunder, it can be a stone of sudden insights and energy shifts.

TWELVE APOSTLES STONE CIRCLE

13. The Outlier Stone

'My energies rise out of the Earth, filling me with joy at so much light, and it rises to join with the layer of bright light over the Earth's atmosphere. Some is siphoned off, and arcs over to the circle, sharing my joy with them.

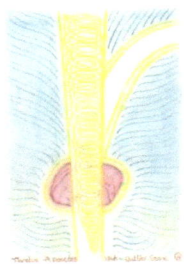

My surface is covered with cup marks to show I am deeply linked with Mother Earth or Gaia. I am a humble stone, very small compared to the rock of the Earth, but I hold quite big energies despite that!'

To look at the stone it is very small, and is only a couple of feet roughly sideways and lengthways. It exudes a strong current of Earth energies that rise constantly through the central area of the stone, about one third of the stone's width. Out of this shaft, the arc of light emerges and is sent over to the Governor Stone, where it joins just above ground.

The source of this vibrant and pure energy of the Outlier Stone comes from an Earth crystal set deep in the Earth, whereas the energy of the Thunder Stone comes directly from the Central Crystal of the Earth itself, as well as the heavens.

The Outlier speaks - 'Why have two sources of energy and not just have the Thunder Stone in this circle? I am providing a constant source of energy in order to keep everything going on a regular basis.

Whereas, the Thunder Stone provides that extra energy which illumines, for this circle is one that brings quite a strong energy for the purpose of gearing people to transformation via the mind, and that is what this circle is about.'

SACRED SITES & PLACES OF POWER
THE SCOTTISH ORACLE CARDS
Element - Air

INSIGHTS OF THE TWELVE APOSTLES

This stone circle specialises in teaching wisdom, and mainly focuses on neophytes, and is a Druid circle. I felt that its old name was something like Caer Alba. The name Beaghmore came up, so possibly the Beaghmore Stone Circle in Ireland is connected to this one. I looked up information about the circle after writing the information above, and found there are stone alignments to the north east of Beaghmore, and so there appears to be a connection.

The Insights
Question. Can you see where a person is on their journey of evolution?
Answer. The Storekeeper Stone (6) – We can see where a person is at, whoever visits our stone circle. *I had felt the attraction of that card coming into my mind's eye.* 'So you can see where I am at?' You are doing well, but not quite finished your soul journey, there is only a tiny bit left, and once that is done, things will start moving. A master is one who has attained this level and is now working in the world to alleviate the problems of others. I wanted to know what the tiny bit was about (!), and was advised to see what the next relevant card will be, at least.

The Evening Star Stone (4) – said to pay attention to the evening star, so I thanked the star and all other stars, including our sun, for all the energy they emanate for our universe. The card asked why I would draw attention to the stars, and I said that the great order of the universe should be known of, in the light of our karmic debts, and by showing our respect to far reaching levels, we help to ease these debts, and it may help towards greater perception of it all. Yes, was the reply.

Q. Is it best to simply ask questions from you, or to obtain the fullest potential of understanding in one's own way; should there be a specific set of questions that could or should be asked in a standard way?

A. The Knowledge Stone (9) – Go around each stone, beginning with the God's Altar Stone, and ask what they hold, to see if further explanation of the gifts as stated can be elaborated on. Then offer information that would be personal to obtain benefit. They can also answer questions on many things other than purely personal information. So ask!

Q. The Knowledge Stone (9) - Concerning the stars, is astronomy of great relevance beyond just knowing when the crops should be planted, or reaped? Are there more sublime uses?
A. My overlighting force or deva strongly links to other realms beyond the Earthly level, and came here in order to create and maintain that link for man's benefit.

Q. How can we feel the closeness of the stars in our life?
A. The Knowledge Stone (9) – Feel that energy that comes through you that has an iridescence and divine peace held in it, which is timeless and unearthly. Through feeling that, messages of meaning begin to filter through to you. Feeling that light flooding in, whether it is day or night, some people who are so filled with it can see in the dark quite easily, or that light comes round them so they can see.

Q. How can we help nature more, in order to fulfil our wishes to see it more natural, prolific and untainted again?
A. The Druid Stone (11) – Go into the still point within. Everyone has their allotted tasks, and yours is to keep on doing what you do, and it will come to the forefront in due course. A book on trees would be magnificent! Each person must look within and see what they can do.

Q. Should people all go to bed early and get up early, or is it ok to do as I do, and go to bed at 1.00 am and get up late?
A. The Harmoniser Stone (3) – your frequency levels are changing, like so many people, therefore we acknowledge that long sleeps or irregular hours are fine. The ideal is to go to bed early and get up early like the sun's hours, this is best in the long run, but if you need to sleep, you must do so, whenever!

Q. Do any beings from other worlds tune in here at this stone circle?

A. God's Altar Stone (1) – Yes, on occasions. If a ceremony or meditation session is taking place here, then they do come by, or to instigate further healing of the Earth. Siriuns, Pleiadeans, Arctureans, Hyadeans, the list is endless! Their intent is in passing on the Universal love, which is of prime importance, and energy for our Mother Earth.

Q. I wish to ask of the duties of the Outlier Stone and where the energy comes from that feeds into the circle, and also about the second outlier found more recently, how it functions?
A. Outlier Stone (13) - The energy you feel comes from down past crystal beds into the depths of the Earth, down to where it gets warm and into a cave that holds the light of the crystalline domains, though visible with the inner eye mainly, and is a link to the underground domain of those Agartha people. Energy pours up and then is filtered off into the circle, much of it soars up and links to that layer of light that overlights the Earth, and is especially visible over circles and sites of energetic power. Yes, the other stone draws energy from below, and sends it all into the circle, though it is less powerful than myself, but plays his part.

Q. Have I even been a high priestess in the past, and if so, what do I need to know in order to fully awaken that now, if I do?
A. The Gatekeeper Stone (5) - Yes, you have a few times, and to know the deeper aspects of the visionquest and working in deep caves are what is necessary to recall your part in the priestess world. Now speak to the kind stone please, for further information.

A. The Kind Stone (10) - I wish to say that you should link to the ancient temples of old, for some still are in the etheric realms, and some exist still in this country too, just try and see what insights come to you. Blessed be.

Q. I asked the circle how best to keep the kundalini energy going well at all times.
A. The Thunder Stone (12) – You felt a little of my energy come into you. Tune into me when you can and things will come to you. When I tuned in again after writing the previous sentence I could feel energy at work in the lowest chakras a lot, and therefore the energy does go to that region. Some kind of

physical exercise helps too, so do more walking! The Earth changes have affected many, including beings and people on the borderlands, who rail against it and pop up to give light workers a hard time.

Q. I asked if any cards wished to elaborate on that, and I did add since there was no response, that my stomach/sacral area feels a bit bloated all the time.
A. The Kind Stone (10) – Your sacral region is in need of more TLC at present, so give it plenty to eat, but not huge amounts all at once. Rest when you need to rest, and give it some healing crystals and massage. If you lie down and fall asleep, you know you needed that quick nap! Even a ten-minute job helps They reckoned I don't relax and rest enough, which is probably true.

Q. I asked if I should do more healing work in the community, or continue with what I'm doing with my creative and seeing work only?
A. The Kind Stone (10) – You are mainly attracted to healing because you, like others, wish to heal, but at a soul and spiritual level you need to heal and self-transform, because you have specific jobs to do, of yet you are still preparing for, and all these cards and codes are preparatory stages, they will help others to prepare too, and all your creative work is geared to that preparation.

Q. What is the ultimate beyond the preparatory stages I'm involved in?
A. The Governor Stone (2) – Your pathway is different, and a place unchartered, and so you have to work your way along in your own way, and your own time, without wanting to linger too long, as time is precious, and you want to know! There are things that will be revealed to you that will help you know what you need to do for sure, the next keys will illumine. As you know, I govern the amount of energy that enters the stone centre circuit, so I am the one that governs. Each person has governing forces at work, knowing when it is ideal to let more of the cosmos in, if it came in before then you would get burnt up or overwhelmed, so, all at the right time is required. Know this, you will become the seer ship you are apprenticed to, and will draw in much that is resourceful for many. Blessed be, from us all.

Suetonius

Suetonius overlights the Twelve Apostles Stone Circle. He speaks here.

'I learnt the ways of the wise many years ago, when the Earth was greener and more pleasantly populated. I wish to say that much knowledge can be learnt here, for I overlight the Watch Stone especially, so link to me here and I can help give insights of Druidic lore and life generally.

I studied the lore to be found in human habitat, as well as nature, and would commune with plants in order to garner their wisdom, both for medical and ceremonial usage. To know how to see into the nature of life itself, so that you can feel at the centre of things, brings its own profundity into your life. Seeking a vision and meditating are both very essential on the path, and seeing the pattern, that is, the warp and weft of the events that happen in life, and to see behind their occurrences, and this will bring much wisdom too, so that you can know causes before events, and the ways to help people on their soul journey.

To be well prepared for whatever life brings to you certainly requires a lot of resources, and that takes time to discover, but keep collecting it, for its value is worthy, and your understanding of it will be too, and so your place in the scheme of things will not be underestimated'.
Blessed be, Suetonius

The History
The Twelve Apostles Stone Circle

This is the largest stone circle in mainland Scotland, and the fifth largest in Britain. The circle is 87.8 x 73.8 metres in diameter, and is a flattened type of circle. Comparable flattened circles in the country are Long Meg Stone Circle and the stone ring at Merrivale, Devon.

It is thought that there originally were eighteen stones in the circle instead of twelve. Four of the stones are boulders, and the rest were quarried, and only five of them are buried in the earth. The tallest is 1.9m high, and the tallest recumbent one to the south west is 3.2m. The tallest stones are to the ENE and WSW. The circle is a plain ring, with no burial cairns within it.

SACRED SITES & PLACES OF POWER
THE SCOTTISH ORACLE CARDS
Element - Water

THE MOTHER STONE CIRCLE

This stone circle, The Mother, can be found along the Glen Almond Valley. The main town as a landmark is Crieff, which lies west of Perth. From Crieff, take the A85 eastwards for about three miles, and at the village of Gilmerton, take the A822 northwards for about seven miles. The parking up the valley called the Sma Glen on the main road is easier than trying to find somewhere to park directly by the Glen Almond Valley itself, although it may be all right to park by the entry gate to the valley. On the ordnance survey map of the area, there is a parking area near the entrance to the Glen Almond Valley, and then the road goes over the bridge that spans the Glen Almond River, and by the bridge on the north side, is the Glen Almond Valley track. A good landmark on the way is the large squarish Clach Ossian stone up the top end of the Sma Glen.

The valley entrance is on the west, and the left side, if approached from the south side. On foot or cycle, travel along the rough track westwards for a mile, until Craignavar farm will be seen. The Glen Almond River runs on the south side of the track, on the left side.

Directly opposite the farm can be seen the profile of the Mother rock, and there is a little wooden footbridge across the river at that point. Go across, and the route to the Mother Circle is easy to find.

THE MOTHER STONE CIRCLE

1. The Mother Stone

She is at the centre of the circle and is the hub of the whole circle's activities, and many a priestess who conducted ceremonies here would mediate between the Altar Stone and the Mother.

There were only priestesses in charge here. There may have been blessed hand fastings, but the men would not have come into the circle itself, but stand outside it, and only allowed in if invited on occasions.

She links to the Source, and also other planetary systems, and awakens that knowledge in priestesses, in preparation for those who will become high priestesses. She knows what is needed at all times, and unlike most circles, she acts as the outlier usually does, for this is an exceptional circle in that way, and she is solid and large enough to act as the capacitator, to safely draw the energy into the circle, but she still has some help from the 'Guides' who act as the governor stone here.

One of her high priestesses from the ancient past was called Ailspaeth, who kept a thought diary, which was full of inspiration, and was to be found by those who could find and perceive its contents psychically. It was to be found below ground, and held within a recess of the rock structure, situated beside the Mother Stone, and it was the Mother Stone's energy that has maintained its existence up to date.

Ailspaeth's diary talks of travelling to Sirius, and the experience can make you see with greater clarity and soul purpose, with intent. There is an overlighting angel that hovers over this Mother Stone, and is Haniel, who helps to keep all in order, and she also helps with energy levels, and to keep the Akashic Record here intact. The kundalini energy can also be balanced by lying next to the Mother; either in person or at a distance is possible. Many people who were wise would come here, and especially the Scots or Gaelic peoples.

THE MOTHER STONE CIRCLE

2. The Seer Stone

'I am at the furthest point up the hillside, on the southern side, and am distinctive for having an eye marked on my flanks. As mentioned by the Guides, I give out a lot of energy from below, and I also link to the Earth like the Mother Stone. My energies, as also mentioned, are partly brought round by the Guides or Governor Stone, having been originally brought up by the Mother Stone.

My energies can stimulate the kundalini and balance the energies within your body, so that the third eye can work for its prime purpose, instead of overseeing the body over and above the minimum requirement.

The symbol on the side of my rocky face denotes the open third eye, and the aim is to get yours to open too, like the high priestess, whose gifts allow her to freely roam to each stone, knowing the qualities and capacities of all.

Whereas, most priestesses only know one or two of the stone's traits, and have to gradually learn them all before they become able to reach the high priestesses level of perception.

I am closed linked with the Prophecy Stone, and our gifts are quite similar, the only main difference is that the Prophecy Stone sees into the future, and I see into the past, and information presently available.

It all depends on who was in the circle at the time, as to whether any were natural Scryer's or not, if so, the high priestess could reside by the Mother and Altar Stones and ask the Scryer to recite her messages, and at other times, when a lot of information was required, they would both be stationed there or at the Prophecy Stone.'

THE MOTHER STONE CIRCLE

3. The Prophecy Stone

'There is one good trademark for a Prophecy Stone, for you will see a pair of upturned eyes within the markings on the stone, displayed on our flanks. Our energies are very vigorous, for we link very closely to the Earth, as does the Seer Stone.

Because I am like a recumbent stone, for I lie still, watching and listening for information from the future, tapping the great Akashic Record, both of the planet and out in the heavens, I look out and up above, searching via the top of my third eye to that information withheld from many. You have to be very still because the information can just come with a flash, and if you don't grasp it all there and then, it will be gone and not easily returned.

So, watch and wait, and know how to slow down in an instant, anticipate the moment when that information will come, and you will be ready. How will you know? You ask. It is when you least expect, when there is a flutter in the breeze, when a ray of light shines on you, a leaf lands on your hand, a tiny or subtle message will let you know, ask for a specific sign if you wish, and you will get it.

In your dreamer moments, both while asleep and your waking moments, things will come to you, so naturally that you hardly know it is prophetic, it is as simple as one day following another, to one who is gifted, and know this, once you frequent a Prophecy Stone, you will bound to become a prophet, mark my words!'

Energy comes up especially to the throat, as well as parts of the head centres, which will enhance the prophetic skills.

THE MOTHER STONE CIRCLE

4. The Ring Stone

Further round from the Fairy Stones you will see the Ring Stone adjacent to the Prophecy Stone. It was given the name, the 'Ring Stone' as couples could be blessed here in hand fasting, with rings or other objects of value placed on top to be blessed, and the stone would bring alignment of good thought power to the couple.

At another level it would be called the Balancing Stone, as it would balance the 'nature' of an individual's chakras and the elements in the body ready for a marriage, so that the usual tensions and discords in a relationship could be superseded as much as possible.

This is a happy stone because couples were expected to take time before rushing into a hand fasting, unlike your present day where it is only too easy to get married, but harder by comparison to break up the marriage.

A year and a day was always the old way of pondering on any given decision for learning, action or experiencing in life, as you would have a full cycle in order to draw the understanding from life, and the ceremonies, and then you would know if your direction would be right or not. The day at the end of the year would be the day when the decision and final conclusion would be enacted.

So, this Ring Stone could encompass more than just hand fasting, it encompasses all major decisions in life and rites of passage. It is symbolised by the large rock representing the year, and the small rock, the day. Some people would be guided to stand next to this stone if they still needed guidance, and their hearts could be strengthened in order to see clearly.

THE MOTHER STONE CIRCLE

5. The Fairy Stones

'These are the stones on the west side, grouped together as a three-some, and they bring in green light and also the capacity for reflection.

"We are situated between the Guides and the Ring Stone.

We bring energy upwards to the third eye, and are called the Fairy Stones because we bring up that essential energy that fairies can use to aid nature".

The fact that the Fairy Stones are at a stone circle means that energy given out from the circle benefits nature especially well, coming from a natural electrical circuit, and we in turn can offer inspiration for those within the circle, for we offer initial links to the shamanic world, for those beginning on the path, as well as us being spokespeople for the realm of nature, and for helping to care for it.

If you link to us, or any other stones that emit green light, it is the sign for 'GO', in order to bring in wisdom about our realm. The fairies that work here wear skirts that emit multicoloured light that is projected out to all life forms in the surrounding area.

Humans can do the same by being a beacon of light shining out their love to all places around them, and carefully tend their gardens with nature's interests at heart before their own!

This they will find out, once they understand the workings of stone circles and other sites, and the spirits that work at these places.'

THE MOTHER STONE CIRCLE

6. The Guides

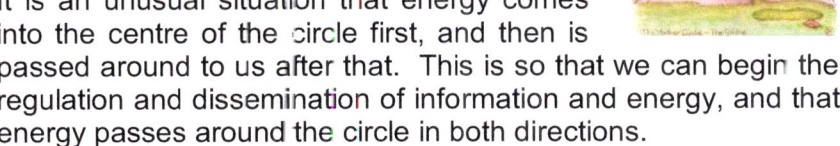

'We are the governor stones of the circle, and are situated to the northern side. We are invited to deal with the energy that the Mother Stone brings in.

It is an unusual situation that energy comes into the centre of the circle first, and then is passed around to us after that. This is so that we can begin the regulation and dissemination of information and energy, and that energy passes around the circle in both directions.

The way in which we can pass energy in both directions, is that there are two of us spirits in the stone, so the western one moves energy anti-clockwise, and the eastern one clockwise, and the energies meet at the Seer Stone on the south side, giving it plenty of energy.

Sometimes it retains the energy for use, and sometimes it is circulated for other stones, or that it returns to us, and we distribute it back again later.

During ceremonies we ensure that energy is kept for requirements, and so if there is a ceremony that requires a lot of information and wisdom given, energy is sent focusing on the Seer and Prophecy Stones, or more for healing perhaps, then it is focused on the Sacred Stones, which are the next ones in the group, and so on.

The Mother Stone duly sends it around for us to distribute, and the high priestesses are aware of all this activity, and inform the circle in advance what type of ceremony is going to take place.

THE MOTHER STONE CIRCLE

7. The Sacred Stones

'We are two spirits, but this time we are situated within two separate rocks that sit side by side, and are originally from one whole stone, as we were when we broke off from the mountain above, but over time we split apart through weathering.

We bring up energy that surges up like a vortex of bright light that is used for healing, and so when healing ceremonies take place, the governor stone or the Guides, as they are called, ensure I have the most amount of energy in order to heal effectively.

We hold much energy, for our stout rocks can absorb a lot of energy, for also, we landed over a good place that resonates well, enhancing our energy.

Sometimes we heal at the physical level and other times at the emotional or mental levels, and at exceptional times the soul level.

So different chakras within our stones are used as a result, and the high priestess will gather my energy to use, as well as direct people to hold onto and lean against the appropriate areas of our rocky surfaces.

This ensures that they stand between our rocky faces because that is where the energy comes up through. These stones are to the eastern side and share the east with the Altar Stone.'

THE MOTHER STONE CIRCLE

8. The Altar Stone

This is situated at the east, just in a more clockwise direction than the Sacred Stones. It is the place of the high seat, where the high priest or priestess in old Celtic circles would be situated.

It is a link to the sylphs, and invocations within the ceremonies were conducted here.

It is a quite lowly flat stone, but this is beneficial, as it acts as a table to place ceremonial items upon.

This Altar Stone and the Mother Stone were often combined as the mediation points, i.e. the central points for the given ceremonies, since the Mother Stone is the central hub of this circle.

The sylphs bring in that air element into the circle, for they work to illumine, and are often brought in where soul searching is required in a healing situation, or for divination, either at the Sacred Stones in the former, or the Seer or Prophecy Stones in the latter case.

'My quiet energy blesses the ceremony and the objects placed on my surface, and any ceremonial food can be enhanced by being left there for a while.'

SACRED SITES & PLACES OF POWER
THE SCOTTISH ORACLE CARDS
Element - Water

THE INSIGHTS OF THE MOTHER CIRCLE

Q. Is there more of Ailspaeth's Diary to be found, and was she a genuine wise woman who lived there? (The diary is something I found when I meditated on the circle one time).
A. <u>The Mother</u> – Yes, she definitely lived, and became the resident wise woman, who lived very close to the circle. She asked 'could I figure out where?' I reckoned on the east side, and I was told it was correct, though no evidence at all is to be found now, for it was a timber hut covered with clay. She put a lot in her diary that could be concentrated on, and more brought out. That would be excellent.

Q. Regarding psychic self-defence, which is all-important, does it differ according to the level you are at?
A. <u>The Seer Stone</u> – Indeed. Although there is the standard methods of sealing chakras and wrapping oneself in light, once the soul clearing begins in earnest, and there are many cords to cut, it is nearly impossible to protect oneself because of this, and vigilant clearings are the only thing to do. Only when it is complete, in the respect of the huge majority of phenomena removed, then protection can be used again, but after a certain level, the light begins to radiate, and that happens once the three lower bodies are entirely clear, and once the heart joins in, the fiery energy automatically ejects any lower astral phenomena from the vicinity if it has not already dissolved on contact.

Q. Could you tell me how my system is in relation to the latter?
A. <u>The Seer Stone</u> – You are well on the way to completion of this condition, even though you may not feel it to be the case. Your sacral is the heaviest place to date, but you are clearing that well, and once that is sorted out, all will be completed. There are always more karmic conditions involved with any soul, but at the immediate soul level lower astral stuff is always finite.

Q. I would say that, knowing some factors for the future is only useful if it inspires a better quality of cultural and spiritual life for the human race, to aspire to, rather than looking for reassurance, and the usual. Are there other useful considerations for being prophetic?

A. The Prophecy Stone - We offer warnings of what might be if certain factors are not heeded, as well as what you mention, inspiration and hope when things are very difficult, to keep the spirit going. I know that people who are older souls do not need this; it is the younger souls who need much encouragement.

Q. If I wished to be an excellent Seer, what must I do to improve?

A. The Seer Stone – Can I ask you which type of Seer you wish to be? There are ones who can see into a person's aura and their guides and associates, or ones who talk to beings such as you do, and can see into the nature of life and know what lies beneath. I answered that I am attracted to both, but not done much of the former in this lifetime. I would say that the latter is your way, and you could give talks about it all when you feel you have enough material to work from, because although you've been doing this for a decade or two, you are only now beginning to access the depth that will be necessary to impart greater wisdom.

Q. I was looking to see if this circle fits an old system, like the ancient Celtic circle, is this correct?

A. The Mother – It partly links in with the ancient Celtic way, but has its own methods, and so is unique, for Mother Nature herself created it, designed for women to use. The Mother is the fulcrum of life, and so is at the centre. The Seer Stone is on the south side facing north, and you have it to your back as you sit inside the circle, so both are facing north. The Prophecy Stone is on the left and the west side, and so it is on the intuitive, reflective side where more right brained activities happen. The Ring Stone is the link between Heaven and Earth, creating balance The Fairy Stones link to the nature kingdom's elementals, adding their wisdom to any insights. The guides are at the north to consolidate wisdom of the great Northern Lodge. The Sacred Stones are at the east where the sun rises, and that sacred light of dawn brings in good energy, and finally, the Altar Stone is where grateful offerings are made, anything from the regular fruits to inner items you wish to change, as well as good energy offered for the circle, and absent healing given out. That sums up this circle's capacity!

Q. What are the full capabilities of this circle, and how women can use it?

A. <u>The Mother</u> – This circle was designed by Mother Nature to keep women's mysteries and skills alive. Although it is not being used much at present, it certainly will be in the future. It is a circle for priestesses, healers, seers, sourcerers, carers, creative women, and many others, for no category is excluded. Just to spend time amongst the stones and feel its love and power is possibly enough for some women. Go to the next stone, she said.

A. <u>The Seer Stone</u> – I help women to see within and develop skills to aid oneself and others, to be perceptive about life and bring depth and insight into proceedings, for without knowing about the reasons why you are here and your soul journey, you cannot be wise and are unable to know how to heal others at a deep level.

A. <u>The Prophecy Stone</u> – Although I am a Seer Stone like the Seer Stone itself, I am able to access the future, which takes more insight as it has not happened, and is not in the Akashic Records. Therefore, I am linked to more subtle realms of perception, including energies, lifestyle, forms of creativity and healing from the future times. I also link to cultures from other planets that will link in to Earth in time.

A. <u>The Ring Stone</u> – It has been mentioned that I oversee any marriage vows, which I do. Yet I am also keen to aid those who wish to unify their consciousness, which means clearing the subconscious, so nothing interferes with endeavours, and the union of Heaven and Earth can take place. This means that the divine energy can merge with the soul or jiva, and the individual becomes a master.

A. <u>The Fairy Stones</u> – We bring the magic that gives a sparkle into that caring role a woman takes, how she tends and cares for indoor plants, that herb garden, the family, pets, and so on. Also she can talk to the nature kingdom as those have done at Findhorn. Blessed be.

A. <u>The Guides</u> – This is the place where the link to spirit guides and helpers comes in, that which helps the woman to find her feet, be her true self, and know how she can draw universal aid into her daily activities, and the gifts she is developing. The northern place of wisdom, though there is wisdom all around for the northern hemisphere the north is the place where all the magnetic energy becomes concentrated, and therefore the Earth's energies are strongest there, and looking to the north, if you are aware, brings that capacity to bear, and so the wisdom from guides can be enhanced by looking there.

A. The Sacred Stones – These stones hold the divine love offered to the circle from Mother Earth, which has come from the Source of all life. This love gently radiates out into the circle, and gives extra strength to women, which heals and transforms those who have had difficult lives up to now, or just feel that a women's lot still isn't a lot. There is an eye above, like with the Seer Stone, and a bit like the Mother, with the diamond inset as in The Guides, showing that The Guides type of wisdom is not far away.

A. The Altar Stone – I am the Altar where all the capacity for transcendence exists, for an altar is a place where sacred objects are placed, tools for healing, all objects and names of people and places, where healing is required. It is a place that is the focal point for ceremonies, and even a person can be laid or sat here at the site itself to give healing. Within the card layout, perhaps a person could be laid with the cards around them You can also bring your concerns, fears, or unwanted traits and leave them at the altar to be cleansed and taken away into spirit, if appropriate. That is it for all the stones! You have it!

Q. I wish to ask about lives in the future, have I had any yet?
A. The Mother – You have already lived in the future times in order to bring through the art that you do, and was formed by communicating with many spirits, also seeing and observing the energies around all life forms. In that time period two hundred years hence at least, all life on Earth will be much changed, and many spiritual groups, galleries and shops will be extant. That is why you are able to focus so well on this task you have set yourself. Once you have done the initial books you have in mind other projects will come up, but you have much to do at present.

Q. Do people still use money two hundred years ahead?

A. The Mother – Yes they do, but because people are much more polite and caring, and there is less need for so many rules and red tape, much has gone and rules are simplified, and there is a growing sense of a wish to allow money to be dissolved in some parts of the world, and there may be an internal sharing or bargaining system in place at home, but still retain the monetary system overseas. Once the Golden Age really kicks in, as some say, the time for some lightworkers will come when they will depart from Earth and move to other more advanced places. Perhaps they will for a while, and return to Earth to offer further wisdom. This will help the planet to move beyond the fourth dimension, and so there will be no going back to the Kali Age, or being immersed in the third dimension again.

Q. Is it true that you can only be a prophet if you've lived in the future?
A. The Seer Stone - More often than not, the person or prophet has, in fact, lived in the future, and of the times he or she may be talking about. The person concerned may have lived on another planet that is more advanced still, which would add even more lustre to Earth.

Q. Have I lived more than one life in the future, and have I lived on another planet?
A. The Seer Stone – You have lived more than once in the future, once in two hundred years hence, and another time shortly afterwards. You have lived on other planets too, and are linked to Sirius, and intend to return there not too long off in the future. I think one more life is in hand, and then you can leave.

AILSPAETH'S DIARY
This is the brief story of Ailspaeth the wise woman of the stones.
"When I was eighteen, I began to see, as a seer should. I could discern how people were, their energy fields, their mien, and so I could help them. I would give them herbs as it reassured them to have something palpable they could use as a medication, relaxant or cheer me up! I could then tell them things that would be perceivable to me.

For instance, people would come about affairs of the heart, and I would help them to be more objective, where objectivity can be difficult. There have been cases where people have come in deep despair because they felt drawn to witchcraft, yet were afraid of what lay ahead, and what they had to do, would they be ostracised by society, and I would tell them it implies a sense of responsibility and inner strength, but not all witches become known to society, for quite a number work on inner levels with spirit, and are therefore not in the public eye.

Tools for witches can be as simple or elaborate as they wish. A favourite stick made into a wand or staff, a cup or bowl for water, a pot to burn herbs to make salves, a garment to use when doing ceremonies. It is the intent that matters most, however, much potency can be sent without all the trappings. Prayers are good, and many can be inspired by what you intend to do.

'Mother of all life, bring riches to bear on me and my kind, and all life around me, may the blessings bear fruit and flourish.'
You can name whatever is specifically required beforehand in the prayer.
There was once an occasion where I got lost. I was a young woman, and of course there were fewer roads and more trees in olden times. It had reached nightfall, being a cold October day, and I had been on an errand on unfamiliar ground. Trying not to get flustered, I took shelter under some pines, as it had started raining, to boot. I had been collecting some materials for my husband who made shoes, as it would save him time, since he could continue some of the manufacturing work meanwhile. As I reached across to pick up something that had fallen from my pocket, for I had bent low to crouch beneath the branches.

I heard a voice, and it said 'fear not, if you follow my instructions, you will reach home safely!' I looked around and saw no one, but then I felt calm somehow, despite that. Waiting for the rain to ease off, the voice began again. 'Walk to that gate on your left.' 'But I can't see anything now, it's too dark!' I replied, and a tear began to come. Suddenly I was aware that I could see the gate, like it had become illumined, and in fact there was a glow around everything. I got up from underneath the branches, and moved in the direction towards the gate. Once through it, the voice told me to follow the illumined route, and it seemed it only took a few minutes before I found myself back at the house.

My husband wondered how I was home so soon, and I told him the story, and I thought I'd been gone for much longer. From that time, the voice became my constant companion, instructing and teaching me much, so that I could give counsel to others, and told me about herbs, where to pick them, and how to use them.

As I learned about the herbs, I began to help others, and the voice, my guide, helped me to know how to also give spiritual help to others. Then, later on, the most difficult lesson came, for my dear husband passed into the light, and one of the most touching things ever was a small parcel I found he had put near my herb collection, and it was a glorious pair of boots he had made for me, and a letter stating how he knew that he would go, and wanted me to have these boots as his parting gift. This all happened when I was in my thirties, and my husband had an apprentice, who decided to take over the shoemaking. I would still go on occasional errands for the apprentice, to collect materials, as well as collecting my herbs, and so I got to know places in the area quite well.

One day I travelled along Glen Almond, for we lived not far away, for I did an excursion to obtain more herbs, and went as far as Amulree for the shoemaking goods, and the local farrier gave me a room for the night in exchange for some herbal treatment. On return, the voice told me to go up the Glen Almond valley for a short way for something of significance would be found. I was thinking of herbs, and so I walked along, the sun shone brightly and I would look at the swift running stream in that, quite wide and flat valley.

As I approached a particular place, a clearing between the tree-line path allowed me a view upon the hillside to the south. A shaft of light lit up a large, squarish rock there, and there were several smaller stones lying around it in a circle. I knew I had to visit it, and somehow clambered over the stream to get there.

'This is the Mother Circle,' said the voice, and my mind became filled with a deep sense of wonder and happiness. "This was where my mother came, and initiated me years ago. She never told me its whereabouts!" 'It is a place where you are drawn to, whether you recall it from earlier time, or a past life or not, it will call you back!' I was very happy.

The full moon and starlight are potent times for linking to the ways of the wise woman. It can be done indoors as long as you can make to contact as strongly as possible, though the real thing is obviously best. This time is best because the daytime holds objective energy for getting material life work achieved. Whereas the night time is for getting metaphysical work achieved. It is also a time for recuperating the body when it is in need of complete regeneration, and it is okay to sleep during the day if only a top up or minimal sleep is necessary, for the night is best, for melatonin levels favour the darkness. The sending out of light can be very effective at night, because the earth is so energetic at that time, and also at dawn just as the sun is arising, the last dose of night time energy, given in a boost before day time comes in.

The circle is a natural protection, as well as an electrical circuit, and therefore enhances all manner of insights, that the wise woman endeavours to find very effectively, and pursues them for others who come to her, as well as for herself, and to know things generally. It is the natural crystals in the many rocks chosen by those who originally made stone circles, or those natural places such as the Mother Circle, which also has crystals impregnated into it, and has a catalystic influence on any circle.

The History
The Mother Circle and Environs

There is no information on The Mother Circle since it is a natural site, and maybe few people know that it exists these days, nor recognise its significance. Situated on the south side of the Glen Almond valley, it occupies a prominent position, and can be easily seen from the track that traverses the valley. There is a feeling of history here, as portrayed in the next paragraph of information.

Within a mile of the entrance to the valley stands Ossian's Stone or Clach Ossian, in the Sma Glen. Ossian or Oisin was the son of Fionn MacCumhaill who was a legendary King Arthur type of figure. Ossian transformed the heroic deeds of Fionn and the Fianna into poetry and song.

Ossian's remains were believed to be in a pit below the stone, and were mistakenly removed, and subsequently taken to the top of Dunmore, a nearby hill, as a piper played. The Fianna were believed to have occupied the hillfort at the Dunmore site. The ashes and urn are now believed to have a Stone Age origin, however, it is a sacred site and deserves respect despite not knowing all the relevant details.

SACRED SITES & PLACES OF POWER
THE SCOTTISH ORACLE CARDS
Element – Earth

THE LOANHEAD OF DAVIOT STONE CIRCLE

The Loanhead of Daviot Stone Circle is found to the north west of Aberdeen, along the A96 main road on the north side of Inverurie, is a direct route.

It can also be approached from the A947 that runs northwards from Aberdeen for nearly eighteen miles, where it joins the A920 near Oldmeldrum.

Take this road, turning westwards for about seven miles, and there will be signposts directed to Daviot, the small hamlet near the stone circle.

The stone circle is found 7km NNW of Inverurie at Daviot village, signposted Historic Scotland, from the B9001 Inverurie to Rothienorman or the A920 Oldmeldrum to Huntly roads.

Once you have parked near the vicinity of the stone circle. The Loanhead of Daviot circle is surrounded by trees, and approached via a footpath for a short distance.

LOANHEAD OF DAVIOT STONE CIRCLE

1. The Altar Stones

"We perform the same functions as at Sunhoney Stone Circle, but we are reversed in this circle. People would come up to the Great Stone to feel enlivened and alert for initiations and ceremonies. You can tune into us any time and we do have much to tell!"

The High Priestess Stone is squat and looks a bit like a Mayan profile head, with its forehead against the central altar stone. It is situated on the left, and is the opposite way around to the Sunhoney Circle, where the High Priestess Stone is on the right side. Out of the stone emanates a fairly narrow spiral with a fast energy, compared with the other emanations, which run straight up into the heavens, or more accurately, the aura of light that surrounds the planet.

The High Priest Stone is another third taller than the High Priestess Stone, and has a fountain-like energy that emanates out of the stone's apex, for it consists of a central column of light with 'branches' that come off sideways from that shaft. The energy actually comes down from that aura of light above and enters the stone, and then shoots back out again to form the fountain of white light.

Like with the Sunhoney Stone Circle, the energy of the High Priestess Stone emanates from the Earth, the energy of the High Priest Stone emanates from the aura of light.

In the centre between the two stones is the **Feminine Energy Stone**, which is a large stone that is the same height as the High Priestess Stone, but is just over twice the width. It has a spiralling energy like the High Priestess Stone, but is twice as wide, so it looks very strong and vibrant. Like the Sunhoney Circle, this stone sits over the natural springs in the area, drawing up that energy in its slow and sure spirals to provide for the wisdom of the Altar Stones.

Message from the High Priestess Stone – "My wellspring energy emanates from a deep cave beneath the surface, and is the home of the Earth Mother, as many caves are. If you feel this energy it will enliven and re-energise you. This energy is sacred, and will transform you too, and even touching this image with closed eyes as you focus, will help the onlooker to receive the energies.

Deep within the Earth lie many leys, and these begin beneath the Earth, and are created via the springs, the igneous rock or huge crystals. All of these emanations are initiated by the elementals and devas of the Earth and they know where the places of exit to above ground level should be placed, for they are just as important above as below ground, for they work in tandem. Below ground the energies work with the Earth itself, the mantle up to the topsoil, but mainly the basic structure of the planet, whereas above ground it is all of life on the surface.

However, as you know much energy seeps upwards from below, joining with ley energies eventually, unless it is part of a ley already. Some leys are just below the ground's surface, and so they work with both levels simultaneously, such as the energy from outlier stones bringing up energy into stone circles."

Message from the High Priest Stone – "I have the energy of star light in my fountain of light, as it comes down from the heavens, entering the Earth's atmosphere. This energy from stars comes into the atmosphere all the time, though humanity is mostly oblivious of it, only the seers of course can perceive this.

The energy is like a wind blowing, in the way that neutron particles move and permeate everywhere. The energy from these stars is then drawn into the huge 'disc' or aura of light that covers many places over the Earth, and especially shines over energy sites, and it then funnels its energy into these sites.

Trees are aware of this and bring down this energy into the Earth, as do people who are awake to spiritual energies, and especially the ones who have an active kundalini energy, or are masters and avatars."

LOANHEAD OF DAVIOT STONE CIRCLE

2. The Teaching Stone

"I am the first stone to the right side of the Altar Stones. I am the Teaching Stone, and I give encouraging energy to inspire and interact with all the other stones.

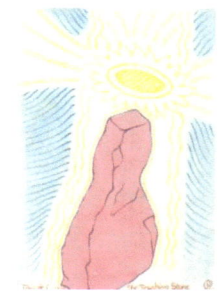

I am the spokesman for the eight stones. I offer joy, wisdom and love, and I am the quintessence of that which you seek. There is a well of energy below us that we maintain. Yes, there is a crystal below us all, quartz, which is tinged with green energetic light."

The Teaching Stone is tall, with a slender area at the top. Above the top of the stone hovers an oval shape like a sunflower head, and a central area with intertwining oval shapes, and a radiant group of petal-like flames around it. This sends out bursts of energy periodically, and that energy inspires whoever comes into contact with this stone, and it was the priesthood who would stand by it in order to inspire others, and in turn would, when training their neophytes, would ask them to stand by this stone especially, in order to enliven their energy fields.

Another part of the energy field of this stone are two wavy strips of energy that come down either side of the stone itself, and start high above the stone. It is a protective energy that is iridescent, and reflects any interference in order to ensure only pure energy is present, that will allow good and true teaching to take place at this site.

The energy that emanates from the sides of this stone's energy fields at the apex, links to the other stones of the circle, and ensures that the energy that the outlier and Altar Stones bring, will travel easily around the circle at all levels, and keeps the frequency high.

LOANHEAD OF DAVIOT STONE CIRCLE

3. The Praying Stone

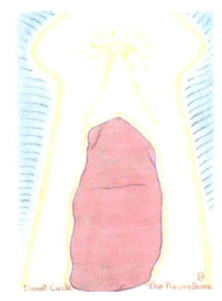

"I am the Praying Stone. Offer to me your wishes, and that opens the way forward.

My energy comes down from that field of light around the Earth, and holds some essence of the energy from the Source, so an eye represents it, surrounded by flame-like petal energies. A white shaft of light radiates from that eye, and is brought down into the stone at its apex. A huge sheath of protective energy comes around the eye and down over the stone, and surrounds it in bright golden white light."

This stone looks solid, and also looks a little like a figure kneeling in prayer with their back to you, and is wearing in a cloak. You can think of it like that if you wish, to bring a human element into it, and in any case, many people did pray by the stones over many millennia.

The energy at this stone comes down and softly surrounds a person, giving warmth and protection, even if not entirely sensed, and that energy will work in an individual's life, over the time that it is required.

It is no coincidence that I am placed between the Teaching Stone and the Guider Stone, for prayers offered will bring in guidance, and also, if the guidance and teaching is good, then the praying is done with greater insight, and a better sense of perspective prevails to bring in what is truly required, and will be done with discrimination.

LOANHEAD OF DAVIOT STONE CIRCLE

4. The Guider Stone

"I am the Guider Stone, and I guide all those who need to find a solution to what course of action is required next. Strangely enough, that may be the reason why those who disapproved of stone circles removed the top of my structure.

My energy uses a balance of heaven and Earth energies, although there are no spiralling energies to be seen, but they run close by below ground, and curiously the energy runs around the stone in arch-like concentric layers, for my shape was roughly conical, and a bit tetrahedron-like, which gave the energy an impetus to give people confidence and determination. It was quite pragmatic, and would help a lot of people in responsible positions, and even seers and healers could receive their visions and insights with a new clarity and alacrity as well.

At the apex of this energy formation, there could be seen two intersecting circles, with a flame-like energy field around it. These intersecting circles link to the realms of infinity, where the physical, emotional and mental realms intersect with the eternal, and take a quantum leap in insightfulness. This energy is the catalyst here.

Use this stone's energy well, to do good works with deliberation and strong intent, and the realms of light will be rewarded, as will your realm.

LOANHEAD OF DAVIOT STONE CIRCLE

5. The Altar Reflector Stone

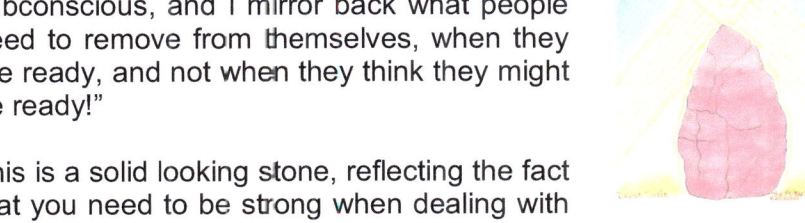

"I am a symbolic representation of the subconscious, and I mirror back what people need to remove from themselves, when they are ready, and not when they think they might be ready!"

This is a solid looking stone, reflecting the fact that you need to be strong when dealing with the subconscious. At the stone's apex there is a double pyramid or octahedron shape, this is the shape for the air element, and so links to the solar plexus and the mind, which is the governing chakra and aspect of the conscious self.

Within the octahedron can be seen the atomic shape, that consists of the three ovals, all gyrating, and there is a sun at the centre of this radiant formation, and so this is of the higher mind and eternal energy, which filters through to the lower Earthly mind and activates the capacity of it to transcend time as it appears to mortal's eyes, and view themselves in a wider scope.

So their subconscious s brought to light, by that light, in order to gently clear it, so that the weight of mortality will gradually lift away, and the nature of eternity then filters in, and becomes part of human consciousness.

This stone is a reflector due to the facility it offers of mirroring the onlooker so that he or she can see themselves more clearly, and also because it reflects the energy that the Altar Stones offer, complementing the Altar Reflector's wisdom.

There are huge energies emanating from the octahedron shape, radiating outwards in all directions, two shafts of energy going up diagonally, and two shafts going downwards diagonally. This energy has a lot of silver in it, and moves quickly to ensure that the reflective capacity works, for the energy field is large and acts as a capacitator for people dealing with their subconscious.

LOANHEAD OF DAVIOT STONE CIRCLE

6. The Dreamer Stone

"I am the Dreamer Stone, and I connect with the dream time, and all that is of higher mind and heart, and I link with other realms and endeavours. I can link energies between one place and another, jump time and space, and hold fast the gateways that could be of value. I especially get the chakras over the head activated."

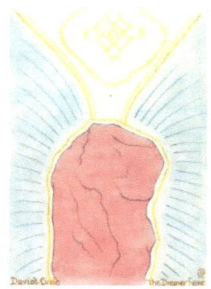

This stone aids those dealing with their subconscious to focus positively on a perspective for the higher mind to consider, so that there is respite from that subconscious, soul retrieval, and individuation process, and in due course the subconscious mind will be cleared, and the person can totally immerse in the dream time unhampered.

In this image, the stone is large and squarish, and has to be because the energies are very high frequency, so the individual needs some ballast in their mien, in order not to become unbalanced when all the head centres are well activated. In the image there is a symbol hovering a couple of feet or so above the stone's apex, and it is of a diamond, with another at the centre, and a flame at each corner, with more energy around, and is surrounded by a wide aura of light. This is the symbol of the vajra, where illumination can be like a thunderclap, and would be the catalyst for higher consciousness offered.

This whole symbol is surrounded by a shaft of white light that emanates from the top of the stone, and it splays outwards as it goes upwards. Equally, energy comes down from the huge disc of light that overlights the planet and into the top of the stone, as well as energy emanating from under the Earth, and filtering through the stone and upwards out of the apex. There is true balance in this link between heaven and Earth, and ensures true and realistic dream power, with potency.

LOANHEAD OF DAVIOT STONE CIRCLE

7. The Adoration Stone

"I comfort and give great peace of mind to those who listen. I offer everything to the heavens, and bring energy from the heavens too, and which governs the atmosphere here, giving healing and inspiration, and it is given to all the other stones as well."

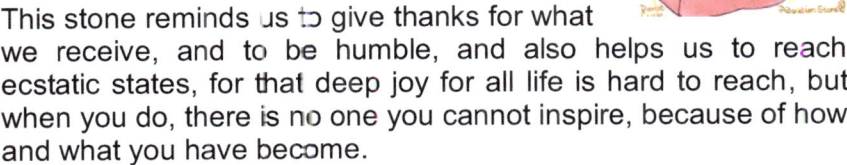

This stone reminds us to give thanks for what we receive, and to be humble, and also helps us to reach ecstatic states, for that deep joy for all life is hard to reach, but when you do, there is no one you cannot inspire, because of how and what you have become.

The energy over the Adoration Stone is a huge ring of light, with a vast disc-like aura, stretching outwards, and from within that ring is a shaft of light that splays outwards as it descends, and all that pure white light encompasses everyone who comes to the stone and receives the beautiful energy given.

The stone itself is very squat, and not very ethereal looking, but it has to be strong since it is to ensure one is grounded while linking to higher energies as they come in powerfully.

This stone reminds you that you must be comfortable in all spheres and states, in the real world of higher states and the same for the physical world, truly balanced and therefore truly able to enter great peace of mind. The energy here helps you to reach that and to see yourself in its truest state, so you can see more clearly how to adjust to this powerful energy.

LOANHEAD OF DAVIOT STONE CIRCLE

8. The Mistletoe Stone

"I was used for ceremonial activities, and mistletoe was placed upon my flanks and the base. Incantations and prayers were said for people who came, who were in need of ritual and ceremony, and they would gather around me, mainly within the circle side, and I would offer my blessings."

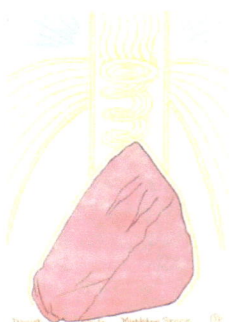

There were places and establishments within the old order that venerated not only the mistletoe for its medicinal and magical properties, but of the sacrificial habits that went with it.

Fortunately, the latter in its base manner was never encouraged here, for not that many druids and pagan minded people practised sacrificial rites in that way; for they would have been well versed in the true soul and spiritual values that would have included harming none. For all life is sacred, and the only sacrifices made would be one's own limitations in exchange for an improved state of being.

The energy here holds an active spiral that emanates from the squat, earthy shaped stone, and gathers momentum a couple of feet above where this spiral becomes a vortex of spiralling energy, that radiates that energy upwards and also out sideways to all of the surrounding area.

A shaft of white light comes down over all of this to the top of the stone.

The stone offers the kind of healing and inspiration that the mistletoe would have, and all manner of protection agencies would have been offered to people in order to benefit, via the rituals and ceremonies, to empower priests, priestesses and aspirants, offering these requirements in the manner in which pagan people and others use rituals and invocations today.

LOANHEAD OF DAVIOT STONE CIRCLE

9. The Ringleader Stone

"I am the Ringleader Stone and I bring powerful energies from the Earth, that is why I am by the female priestly stone of the Altar Stones, and I connect with the previous stones, especially the Adoration Stone, to balance energy in the circle.

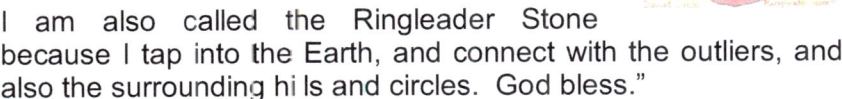

I am also called the Ringleader Stone because I tap into the Earth, and connect with the outliers, and also the surrounding hills and circles. God bless."

This stone is like other stones I've come across in other circles, which also link with Earth energies, and bring that energy into the circle. There is usually one of this type of stone within every circle, and I have known them as the 'Governor Stones' even if they have been given another name.

That is the best name for them really since they govern the amount of energy that enters a site, and they share that capacity with outliers, for they are also capacitators of energy handling and distribution.

The image shows the tallish and broad stone with a huge and measured spiralling energy emanating from the ground. It totally encompasses the stone, and the shaft of light around the spiral surrounds everything, and that spiral energy draws from the outliers below ground, drawing the energy up into the circle.

Some of the energy, like all the other stones, links en masse to each other at the apex of the circle, and that apex holds the image of an eye and a shaft of light there, to show that the energy of the site is wide awake and active.

SACRED SITES & PLACES OF POWER
THE SCOTTISH ORACLE CARDS
Element - Earth

INSIGHTS OF THE LOANHEAD OF DAVIOT STONE CIRCLE

Q. I wish to ask what the true name of this circle is?
A. The true name is Cairnbreagh.

Q. What is the speciality for this circle? Also the qualities and characteristics for learning purposes for the apprentice wise woman?
A. <u>The Altar Stones</u> - It is a Gateway. In other words it is an entry point to different worlds. This particular gateway specialises in healing the soul.

Q. Can you see how I can begin to clear my sacral area?
A. <u>Teaching Stone</u> – There is something you must do before this can be sorted out. (I did some inner clearing). There is a symbol you must focus on for a day or two, and then after a break, have another session. (I was given the symbol of two intersecting ovals and to see it at the sacral region.)

Q. What caused the closure of the sacral?
A. <u>The Guider Stone</u> – It is a coincidence that this stone was broken out of all the others, as it was a woman's link to her own power. You have a fair chunk of power held in abeyance, and this was due to power abuse many hundreds of years ago, which you have forgotten. You have given away quite a lot over the years, so you don't need to do too much there. You have to just await its stirring into action, but meanwhile, consider bright orange colours and peach, as well as gold and the symbol of the spiral, and that's it! You have done well to persist when you are so tired, stop and rest my friend, blessed be.

Q. Is there a particular spirit who lives here?
A. <u>The Altar Reflector Stone</u> – This stone is ideal as it reflects on the energy given at the Altar, and complements it, and is therefore a good place for a resident spirit to speak from, who originally lived and worked here. 'My name is Golaneth, and I was the high priest here, and there is also a devic presence

called Aultun, and the word means 'the ancient spirit of the place', and could be extended, but is usually abbreviated as such, being Auldweighndun, but sounds ponderous so is shortened. He usually has no place and moves about the stones freely. We understand the human soul very well.

Q. Given the nature of soul retrieval, and can be either all at once or in several life times, does a person have to have passed particular initiations for it to start, and in a reflective lifestyle?
A. The Dreamer Stone – The soul retrieval work comes from the soul's wish before incarnation, and only once the heart is well open and the inner strength is resolved enough to withstand the impact. When all the bodies of the personality are stable to the right degree, then it is the time of completion, the autumn of the personality, and the spring of the cosmically inclined soul to enter another stage of self-development, which becomes selfless, since the lower self begins to fade away.

Q. Can a person in soul retrieval need really use these cards well to help themselves, or will they need more guidance from myself etc., in case they do not have clairsentience skills?
A. The Adoration Stone – You will find that most soul retrieval people already have adequate clairsentient skills, as they have to be so, in order to experience soul retrieval. It all depends on their skills, and you may wish to include soul retrieval pointers for use. Check our different qualities and that will give you the key.

Q. Are there women's rites and methods of working that will enhance her power from a soul retrieval point of view?
A. The Mistletoe Stone – There is a lot that can be done, and is a question of doing a lot of inner work and reflection for things to come to the fore. Mistletoe was sacred to the Druids, and you need to look at that more, for it holds things that have been concealed for a while, and more than just a peck at Christmas time! The herb aims to bring about union within oneself, and with the Goddess. I then felt that flying ointment might be an herb like mistletoe, and Ayahuasca and similar.

I then felt that the flying ointment might be a blind to obscure that they may take a 'flying substance' that might have the same effect as mistletoe, and also be like Ayahuasca and similar.

Q. I wondered about women's mysteries and awakening methods.
A. The Ringleader Stone – I feel has the energy having experienced the energies of the Mistletoe Stone. Yes, look up information on women's mysteries, and see from there what else needs to be asked, and return again for a session with us stones, blessed be!

That finished the sessions, but felt inspired to go around all the cards and tune into them energetically, and see what comes of that.

1. The Teaching Stone – I just felt the energy, sunny and bright.

2. The Praying Stone – I felt sunny energy streaming down and filter down the meridians to my feet.

3. The Guider Stone – I felt the energy working at my throat and hence the sacral region.

4. The Altar Reflector Stone – I felt a deep sense of peace, and a feeling that it would strengthen the system on the subtle levels, and had silver or gold, or both, energies coming in.

5. The Dreamer Stone – I felt very peaceful, especially felt energy focusing at the third eye.

6. The Adoration Stone – I felt great peace coming in at the crown.

7. The Mistletoe Stone – I felt good energy all round.

8. The Ringleader Stone – This immediately worked with my base and sacral regions, and also the Alta Major.

9. The Altar Stones – These stones worked with all the chakras simultaneously.

I chose a selection of the stones I felt would benefit me the most, being the numbers 3, 4, 8 and 9. I worked through the auric levels.

The Guider Stone – All was very gentle, and a sense of reconciliation to a small degree as not much to do, and the synthesis of that. I also felt very sleepy.

The Altar Reflector Stone – I felt a degree of energy around me and down to the feet, when I concentrated on the central symbols within the diamond.

The Ringleader Stone – I felt the energy at work again, though not as strongly as initially, (as with the other stones) so usually means their work has been done.

The Altar Stones – I did not feel much on this occasion, and only a bit at the mental level.

<u>The History</u>
The Loanhead of Daviot Stone Circle

It is a well-preserved recumbent stone circle, and one of the best of its type. The circle is elliptical, and is based on a near Pythagorean triangle. Its origin has been dated to 2,200BC, and it is the only known date. The site was levelled before it was built upon. There is a ring cairn in the middle, and it was used for funerary purposes, and possibly built later than the stone circle. There was possibly a timber mortuary house built before the central ring cairn.

The diameter of the stone circle is 20.5 metres, and it is sited near the top of a wooded hill on the north side of the village, and there are views to the east and south.

There are eight standing stones, one recumbent stone and two flankers. There are cup marks on the stone beside the east flanking stone. Each of the standing stones was put over a small cairn, which contained charcoal and potsherds.

There are two stretches of low rubble bank to the south east, forming arcs of equal length on opposite sides of a circular area.

There was a Bronze Age site nearby, enclosed by a bank and ditch, and contained cremations and remains of thirty people, placed in urns or small pits.

There was also a hearth found in the ring cairn in the centre of the stone circle, and perhaps the site had been used as a dwelling place when the site had lost its meaning as a sacred site, or it may have been used as a ceremonial hearth.

SACRED SITES & PLACES OF POWER
THE SCOTTISH ORACLE CARDS
Element - Fire

THE EASTER ARQUOITHIES STONE CIRCLE

The Easter Arquoithies Stone Circle is found to the north west of Aberdeen, as well as the Loanhead of Daviot Stone Circle.

This circle is situated along the A96 main road on the north side of Inverurie, and is a direct route.

On approaching Inverurie from the south, there will be two roundabouts en route. Go directly across the first one to the south side of Inverurie.

Once at the second one to the west side, turn left onto a small minor road, and travel along it for about a mile to Burnhervie.

The stone circle is three miles west of Inverurie, and will be found via the Historical Scotland signs signposted from the A96 Inverurie bypass.

EASTER ARQUOITHIES STONE CIRCLE

1. The Altar Stones

On the right side, the energy of the Priestess Stone draws up her spiralling energy from within the Earth. It runs through the stone and goes up a shaft of light into the disc of light, or auric layer that  surrounds the planet, where it links with all the energies of each stone at the apex. A ring of cleansing power runs vertically up and down the shaft, strengthening that energy when required. This is where the high priestess stood, and would receive this strong Earth energy to enliven herself in order to give of her best, and also so that she could speak well in wisdom and counselling, as well as healing.

This Earth energy comes up from granite that lies deep below, which radiates that energy outwards. The spiralling motion is as a result of the pulsating dragon or serpent power of the Earth, though the pulsations here are of a high enough frequency, so they aren't as distinguishable as they would be if somewhat slower, but can be in other places, such as mentioned in the next paragraph. The rate of pulsation will naturally denote the frequency level at a site, and a faster rate is more favourable for visionary work and higher frequency healing, and the higher chakras. The comparatively slower rate would be good for a peaceful and restful energy where de-stressing fast moving chakras or energising the lower chakras is required.

The stone between the priestess and priest stones also has a spiralling energy, but this is a big wide spiral, which is slower, so its frequency is much more grounding, and could be called on for other requirements, such as healing where slower vibrations could calm, and bring in clearer thinking if a person was agitated, maybe even take a person into a trance state for various reasons, both for inner work in a hypnosis capacity or for astral travel.

The priest stone has energy coming down into the apex of the stone, a strong vertical shaft, and as a result of that, four shafts of light radiate out of its apex and arc outwards to either side of the stone. This energy radiates strength for use in promoting strength of character, enhancing bravery, and operating under difficult circumstances, for all was not as peaceful in their world at all times. The high priest had equal status as the high priestess, and they would enact ceremonies together. He would offer his power and strength when she was 'working', and she would offer her divine wisdom and visionary powers when he was 'working'.

The central stone appears to have the best of both priest and priestess energies as a result of being between the two stones, and in a way this is the case, even though it has its own energy, drawing up from below, from a slightly different part of the rock or granite, that has a slower frequency level. The ancients perceived these energies were underneath the ground, and depending on the shape and size of the stone that they placed above ground, its own character would take on and modify the energy accordingly.

EASTER ARQUOITHIES STONE CIRCLE

2. The Scryer Stone

I link to the heavens via the third eye, and that cosmic antenna commonly known as the crown chakra, and it includes the ones above that too, if possible. As shown by the eye at the apex, which also indicates the Source from where much information can be gleaned, as well as being a catalyst for greater insight and understanding.

The plume-like flame shape above, relates to the crown, solar star and stellar gateway chakras, being all open and appearing like a great antenna, and also this is reflected in the Egyptian Pharaoh's head dress, a bishop's hat and even the conical hats witches and wizards wore, and some American Indians, the Paiutes, have worn them, for they all reflect the general shape.

The energy then emanates from the centre of this eye, and encapsulates the stone below in a wide tepee-shaped structure of light.

Within this area a gifted psychic, priestess or priest, and visionary, could stand and find the enhanced energy tailored for scrying, to aid whatever insights the person would portray during a ceremony.

'Many an insight gained' is what I feel has been the case, when people used this stone in the past.

EASTER ARQUOITHIES STONE CIRCLE

3. The Inspirer Stone

This stone links to the East where the high seat in the ancient Celtic system is found. The energy here is fairly fiery, for there is a brightness to be found.

The nature of the energy over the stone is like three fountains, all emanating out of the stone, and becoming larger as they progress higher. This energy is not spiralling, but is coming out of the ground like this because it is emanating from underground water that runs over rock that radiates energy the way igneous rocks do, such as granite, hence the fluid looking energy patterns.

The fiery strength of that energy will be because of the granite being igneous, and I could feel its power coming through my feet.

The high priest would have dominion at the east; the 'elevated chair', and this fiery energy would be that illumination to be expected at the centre of the Celtic Awen of Druidic practice.

The fountain structure is also like three chalices, reflecting the watery element as well as the earth and feminine, but its fiery presence, and reaching upwards and outwards also links it to the air element, which is the true dominion of this eastern direction.

So, all the four elements come in here, which gives this Inspirer Stone a force that is well balanced, and only to be expected for an elevated state of the high priest or priestess stature.

EASTER ARQUOITHIES STONE CIRCLE

4. The Wisdom Stone

This stone has a kind of pristine quality to it, in that I could see a washbasin and bath with suds to indicate that this stone prepares or purifies an individual or neophyte in order to allow the wisdom easier access.

In this process of preparation, there is the usual clearing, emotional, mental and psychic, soul and spiritual levels, which can be a lengthy process, where all of the subconscious is seen for what it is, a mass of collected ways of thinking, attitudes and opinions.

A lot of this may be outdated, and subconsciously influences your daily life, and the only way to clear it is to remember, and by doing so, the potency of it is nullified.

Some memories are easily removed, others are a little emotional, and a certain percentage are very upsetting and are in knots, tangled amongst other life memories associated with it, and take the most time to clear, as there also tends to be various levels involved.

As well as clearing, relearning ancient wisdom and bringing it into your life, reclaiming your skills from all time is a positive step to take while preparing yourself, your new you! Or is it your ancient and modern or timeless you! There may be skills you once knew, or even new wisdom techniques that hasn't been seen before on this planet.

Energetically wise, around this stone the main feature is the eye in the centre of a diamond, with a flame at each corner.

The eye links to the third eye, the Source and active wisdom, and the diamond is the link to higher wisdom and spiritual levels, and the four flames link to spirit and to transmutation.

The shaft of brilliant white light comes down from above, around the eye and diamond, and then deep into the Earth.

EASTER ARQUOITHIES STONE CIRCLE

5. The Initiation Stone

This is a significant stone because when all the individuation process within has been completed, and no more past life information is left to disturb the equilibrium, then you would move to the Initiation Stone in order to receive the energy of renewal.

You are then initiated into the Brotherhood of Initiates, and the inner eye is awakened and will remain so in other lives to come.

The energetic form around this Initiation Stone consists of two conical energies. The first one is of a cone-like shaft above the eye, bringing energy to illumine the inner eye.

The second cone is of energy and light emanating from the pupil of the eye that radiates down over the standing stone.

This is the energy gained from inner insights that can begin to be radiated or channelled from yourself out into the world.

I sense that this stone can draw energy from the individual, not to deplete, but to make the person able to radiate energy rather than just be a recipient.

There is a gradual opening out of understanding, knowledge and wisdom from the higher worlds that come into the person's life.

The energy emanating knows where to go, in order to act as a catalyst for all these changes, and also provides a shawl-like protective covering over the initiate as he or she grows into this new-found state of being.

EASTER ARQUOITHIES STONE CIRCLE

6. The Saintly Stone

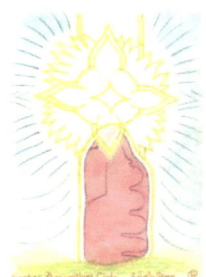

A shaft of light descends to the stone from above, and at the apex of the stone there is a four-pointed star, with four large flames, one at each corner, with a fiery mass of energy around the whole structure.

This symbolises the powerful energy available when the crown and other head centres are open, and inspiration has a free reign in an individual's life, as well as linking to God consciousness, Goddess, the Source, and all the beings on higher levels.

This stone is used for those who are to be initiated as high priests or priestesses, as well as those who are aspiring masters.

The star at the centre denotes the ability to contact intergalactic beings and forces that initiate or enliven cultures of the human race.

The light is brilliant and only able to be withstood by those who are ready to receive it, and all others will be repelled, but not uncomfortably, just not able to link in well enough to understand what it is about, and feel disinclined to investigate.

There are many different colours of the spirit world on offer here, metallic shades and golden hues, all with iridescent glows.

A direct link to the Source via external timeless states takes place here as well.

EASTER ARQUOITHIES STONE CIRCLE

7. The Grounding Stone

This is the stone that links very deeply into the Earth and brings the riches of that energy into the circle, and also up into the apex of the circle's collective energy.

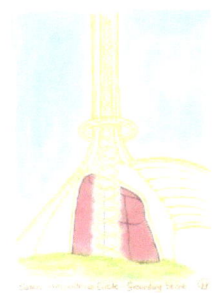

As well as the depths of the Earth, the energy also comes from the mountain of Bennachie, which lies to the south west, and also from a hill fort to the north west called Dunnideer.

The latter site has much crystalline sources below it, and simply pours energy out of it, upwards.

The type of energy shown is the characteristic spiralling action, which shows it is pure and self-cleansing as it moves and flows. There is also a ring of energy around the shaft as it rises out of the stone to the apex of the whole circle's energy.

This ring is to be found at the apex of the stone itself, and there is a halo of light around the whole stone, and the shaft of light coming through the stone is very broad as it goes through the stone, and in fact, splays out beyond the halo just to reveal its power.

Some of its energy goes out to stone number seven, and the energy enters the circle underneath the stone.

This stone comes after the Saintly Stone because it is part of the order of sequence, to ground and give out energy and illumination given to an initiate once received.

This is because that energy is meant to be shared to transform the world around you, and not just kept to him or herself; this is not a true Mastership trait!

This giving out of energy, skills and wisdom is an essential step in soul and spiritual growth, in order to prove that you are a true high priest or priestess, or even a master, and once successfully done, one can only then make further progress, perhaps on different planets!

EASTER ARQUOITHIES STONE CIRCLE

8. The Effulgence Stone

This stone shows the energy as radiant and pouring out on all sides, and some of the energy is exchanged with the grounding stone, number six in line, where energy comes in, and in doing so, it catalyses the Effulgence Stone, which aids it to pour out light.

This outpouring of light and energy is comparable with the Mastership achieved by those who attained to resonate with the Saintly Stone, and then prove their worth at the Mastership or Grounding Stone.

Now at the Effulgence Stone their energies increase once more, so that their capabilities rise beyond that of human consciousness as we know it, and know none of that any more, simply bright peace filling every atom of their bodies.

There is not a trace of anxiety, worry, human problems, fears and so on, simply a clear-sighted knowingness of why they are on Earth, and the intent to help other people with no interest in their own selves.

This is because the personality has been absorbed into their higher selves and become one with the atmic body, and so they are attuned and in unity with divine consciousness.

The joy of such shines through so radiantly that they cannot help but show it through the glow in their eyes, love in their hearts, and the extreme dedication to helping others as they can see into all the hearts on the planet, and have now become truly planetary guardians.

Like the Effulgence Stone, these ascended masters also do the same, and whether incarnated or otherwise, for it is their choice to do what they need to, their auric field is a radiant mass of healing energy, much sought after, and offers profound healing and transformation to many.

EASTER ARQUOITHIES STONE CIRCLE

9. The Sage Stone

The Sage Stone offers an ability to see into other states of being on more advanced worlds, and to see the destiny of planets and galaxies as well as of Earth herself. Having served thoroughly in the world, there can be 'time out' in order to contemplate deeply, and at certain times that information can be given out to others, but they will seek the individual out, rather than the master go to them, because he or she is at a stage where contemplation and inner seeing are necessary.

As well as that, they send out healing light to many, and all places around the planet, knowing where it is expedient to send it, not to interfere in karmic experiences people have to endure, but to ensure stability of the planet is maintained, and things don't get out of control.

The energy here is like a huge diamond encompassing the stone, so spiritual energy is here present, and within that diamond there is a smaller diamond that encompasses the apex of the stone.

From the four points of the smaller diamond, an effulgence of light emerges that splays outwards with a convex shape around the edges, and is surrounded by what looks like nine petals or flames. For, although there is a fruitful flowering of energy, it also holds the strong flame of spiritual energy in it too, shown through the element of fire.

This energy looks to have a discipline and an exactness in its nature, for it is echoed in its structure. It is also very still, and would be very trying for many in this restless world, but would produce rewards for those who wish to make use of its positive characteristics and the gifts it would share.

A remote cave hundreds of miles away from anyone and anywhere would be the ideal location for the contemplative side of things, in order to take advantage of this stone's nature, but those who aspire, inspired by the ascended master can create that environment wherever he or she chooses!

EASTER ARQUOITHIES STONE CIRCLE

10. The Searcher Stone

This Stone has a strong flame-like energy around it, and above that, energy streams out like mist of clouds soaring upwards from the peaks of Kachenjunga or Everest.

Other energies are apparent lower down that emanate in parabolas, and increase in size as they progress up the stone's flame-like energy field. This energy looks free to move wherever it will, as if unencumbered by gravitational forces, both physically and spiritually.

The individual is now free to roam wherever he or she will, not sequestered in a cave-like environment as with the Sage Stone, but can now be attuned to the 'winds' that blow from other parts of the galaxy.

As a result they can see with the eyes of an advanced being who understands the ways of living on planets much more wise than ours, and can ground that understanding into the Earth, as shown by the chalice with spiralling energy around its stem, with a four-petalled flower and a square shaped centre.

The square echoes the Earth and the four petals for the four elements. At the centre of the square centre there is an eye, once again it reflects the Source, and that supernal link with no time, unity consciousness, and the ability to see deeply and bring that wisdom into everyday consciousness.

The title of Searcher Stone denotes the ability of the initiate here to seek, and to know where to look for whatever information and wisdom that is available in our universe, and to know that all is obtainable, as well as that deep stillness, as mentioned, in the Sage Stone.

For it is a combination of these types of energy that can be accessed, which culminates with the result of this freer energy at the Searcher Stone.

SACRED SITES & PLACES OF POWER
THE SCOTTISH ORACLE CARDS
Element - Fire

INSIGHTS OF THE
EASTER ARQUOITHIES STONE CIRCLE

The energy at this site is definitely fiery. Not the fire by friction, but spiritual fire, where energy moves and stimulates, but is not hot or cold. It rises from the Earth and brings succour to many, even if they are not aware of it.

Q. How is it possible to live in a world that has a lot of low frequency energies around, from places, people and objects?
A. The Scryer Stone – It is difficult for higher frequency people, as they always have to be on the look out. For those who are moderately higher, it is fairly simple, but when objects, as well as energy lines, buildings, people, and all this locally and even at a distance too, and then it all has become almost a full time job to constantly adjust to requirements. The dwelling has to be constantly vetted, and only then can you find out what to do next. Simplicity helps, and regular tuning in to your crystals and guides to ask what may need attention next, for clearing the house etc., say once a month for instance. People eventually reach a stage when they can become impervious to entities, houses and everything like that. Learning about dowsing will help!

Q. What is it like to be a Master?
A. The Effulgence Stone - It is a bit like my energies, where I radiate rather than holding it around myself, either coming into the system or flowing away. With a Master, energy radiates, and this comes when all the chakras are open and receptive, and energy enters the heart and the sacral, and radiates outwards, for nothing much is there to stop it radiating, which produces a natural force field to keep any unwanted energies in check. That is it in a nutshell. You will want to know how to get like that, no doubt!

Q. How does a person attain this radiance of energy?
A. The Effulgence Stone – It requires a lot of balance between the five elements, to ensure one is not overly lacking, and can be

seen in birth charts. Being out in nature helps, and if you can't get out, have the elements around you, with crystals, water in bowls, candles, and so on

Q. What does this stone circle group represent within the context of these five sets?
A. <u>The Grounding Stone</u> – This circle offers a fine-tuning, in order to establish as much balance as is possible and relevant, in order to deal with very high frequencies, and also the very low ones. For this attainment is a Mastership skill. <u>It would be beneficial to go around each card</u>, taking note of what each says, and the comments and advice they give in order to consider them.

1. <u>The Scryer Stone</u> – May the eye be pure, and then the light is free to enter, unrestrained. Be pure! Know it in your heart. If you have to question, you don't know it. It is when your heart is filled with peace and love constantly.

2. <u>The Inspirer Stone</u> – Let the triple layers indicate the pure channels of the higher chakras over the head, as well as purity of thought, word and deed. Also the physical, mental and emotional layers, so you can be truly inspired!

3. <u>The Wisdom Stone</u> – This stone offers a peaceful balance, for the diamond of spirit links with nature to show the green light. The eye is open and the four flames and elements show transmutation and a sublime link to peace. Are you ready? (You almost are, so keep progressing.)

4. <u>The Initiation Stone</u> – 'There is more green energy given here via the open eye, with energy brought from the heavens, the cosmos, Divine Mother and Father, and the Source, to activate good energy, to bring in that cosmic energy into your midst, so you can offer what you know to the world.' I felt one part of the ray from the eye go to my heart, and other parts to the crown and the sacral regions.

5. <u>The Saintly Stone</u> – When I looked into this image via the third eye, I saw images that were ever-changing, of kundalini and caduceus, cross-like and Celtic strap or knot work, all vibrant and radiant, and was radiating that energy to me. 'The richness of

this card can never be underestimated. Do look at it frequently and write your findings.' *

6. The Grounding Stone – I felt the energy coming from this stone's image as very peaceful and loving, and also strengthening, and immediately I felt it must be used in conjunction with the Saintly Stone. 'After doing soul retrieval, one is like an emerging entity from a chrysalis, and need more strengthening in order to deal with the heavier energies all around oneself.' *

7. The Effulgence Stone – 'Within this stone is the secret of becoming an effulgent being. Take note of me, and you shall perceive and achieve! Blessed be!'

8. The Sage Stone – I felt the diamond-like waves of white light washing through my aura. 'This card is the light house of the pack, the radiant 'shower of the way', so that you can meet the needs of those who wish to know about higher frequency levels.' *

9. The Searcher Stone – I felt the wide-ranging nature of this card, but I am not sure what the searching culminates with! 'This card links to other realms and regions, so try it and see!' *

10. The Altar Stones – Find out what the true meaning of an altar is! If it is within you, you don't need the altar, but an outward show can be a representation for what is within, like all creative work, it shows you your yardstick, your measurement on the scale of life's frequency levels! See and find out what it truly means. *

* All these cards I would link to in the next session.

5. The Saintly Stone – (I was invited to look at this card on frequent occasions).
'Abandonment of the Realms of the Past', was a phrase that came. Not just my own, but helping the world to do the same, I felt was relevant. It often works hand in hand, our own direct experience aiding one's service capacity. The energy is balanced as Heaven and Earth are linked, creating a capacity for unity, and also in anyone who links in. Energy was descending with this card.

6. <u>The Grounding Stone</u> – The energy in this stone links Heaven and Earth, but the predominant force of energy is going up, due to the quickly spinning spiral energy. At the physical and etheric level, I felt energy activating at my base and sacral. I also felt energy going to my throat at the mental level.

8. <u>The Sage Stone</u> – It is a symbol and actual energisation of final stages of earthly life. It balances the individual's energies so that they are perfected to an 'Earthly' degree, i.e. while on Earth. The four points are the four elements and the fifth of ether has its place in the centre, within the diamond. At the physical and etheric, and the emotional levels, I felt the sacral and throat areas needed more energy, due to the menopausal state finalising itself, and the clearing of ancient sites etc recently. Not too bad, considering.

9. <u>The Searcher Stone</u> – I feel that the card searches for the grail energy held within you (if you haven't already found it!). The grail image is the chalice with its spiral pool/eye image at the centre, and four petals linked with the base chakra, and it is also grounded in the four elements. I concentrated for a while, and then having had little results, I got the words 'Find what you seek!). I then felt an acceleration of energy, and as if activation was progressing in the sacral and base areas. I then felt the energy all pervading through me, like a unifying link with Heaven and Earth, very peaceful.

10. <u>The Altar Stones</u> – As I concentrated, I felt a beautiful feeling of timeless peace, very strong peace pervading my aura, so that I could feel the Altar Stones give that feeling of the unity of Heaven and Earth via the energy coming from the Heavens via the masculine stone, and the feminine Earth energy from the feminine stone, and spiralling energy from the stone between them. So the altar energy should be like this, for any altar you create in order to create or facilitate this transcendent energy to come to your own altar, and even better if it comes within yourself, for that is the ultimate. I must try these cards again – no's 5,6,8,9, and 10.

5. <u>The Saintly Stone</u> – The grail energy is felt in the head or mind here, so it is not just in the sacral, or just in the head, it is all inclusive, and you become like a conduit for deep wisdom,

understanding, Earth Mysteries and the Goddess, and much more. How to achieve this, by being truly humble, with a wish to know, and a sense of wonder at life, as well as deep reverence and respect.

6. <u>The Grounding Stone</u> – This stone helps a person stay focused on what they wish to achieve, keeping unwanted influences at bay, ensuring that an objective or goal that is wished to achieve, is not left to dissipate by life's forces. This stone will strengthen resolve. I also felt a link between the base and crown centres, brought closer with this card, and brought in a definite unity in respect of the angle of balancing and grounding.

7. <u>The Effulgence Stone</u> – The card shows three points where energy radiates from, from the top and the two sides as shown, and may of course relate to the other two sides as well. I asked about its nature, for those who come, abundant energy could be for those who wish for it. In order to radiate energy constantly, you need to have much energy coming in. Like someone who has abundant food, they have plenty to give away, or advice skills too, those who don't have either cannot give! You have to have the faith that it will come to you at the right time.

8. <u>The Sage Stone</u> – This stone is best described as a feeling of balance and harmonising capacity. It had more effect at the mental level, where the diamond and the four quarters of north, east, south and west, are the balancing of the elements, the image became a shining white equilateral cross, with those halo-like fiery flames at the end of each arm, a fiery cross indeed, and so it included the ethers of the spirit.

9. <u>The Searcher Stone</u> – At the physical/etheric level I felt stimulation at the base chakra, which is especially beneficial having not been well recently. At the emotional level I saw the grail cup brimming with white light, and it radiated outwards to my base and throat chakras. I felt as if it was trying to indicate things that will 'well up' for future activities, gifts etc. At the mental level I felt energy permeate me all throughout my system, like with the energetic flow as shown on the card from the top and right side.

10.   The Altar Stones – I felt energy flow through me, and I compared it with the Effulgence and Searcher Stones. I asked what the best of the Altar Stone capacities would serve as a hierophant's requirements. I was told that inspired speech, bringing through what comes, is of great importance, specific and highly attuned information. Understanding paths that people require, what their needs are, not what you think they might be or assume they are. Emotional level – being in touch at higher levels, the higher selves, so can bring unity and deeper understanding of people's needs, and things can be picked up there. Mental level – the vision will come for hierophancy, for self and others' development.

The History
Easter Arquoithies Stone Circle

The name of this stone is pronounced Easter 'Ah Whawrthies'. This is one of a number of recumbent stone circles found in the Grampian region. It consists of nine upright stones, one large recumbent stone and two flanking stones or flankers. There are some diamond shaped and some narrower stones like at the southern avenue at Avebury.

It was built during the early phase of Neolithic Stone Circle development. The stone was brought from the Don Valley six miles away, as stone wasn't available locally. Some stones were of a reddish granite, others a grey granite. There are a few of porphyry and one of jasper. Unusual!

The circle diameter is 19.5 metres and is a perfect circle, and there was an internal cist and ring cairn put in latterly. It is on a hillside site.

SACRED SITES & PLACES OF POWER
THE SCOTTISH ORACLE CARDS
Element - Ether

SUNHONEY STONE CIRCLE

The Sunhoney Stone Circle is found to the western side of Aberdeen, along the A944 main road that runs due west out of the city.

It passes through places such as Kirton of Skene, Dunecht, Alford and Bridge of Alford, for reference.

To find the stone circle, travel along this road to Dunecht, and turn southwards along the B977 to the crossroads at Echt.

Turn right or westwards from there along the B9119 for just under a mile, and it will be found nearby.

It is approached along a footpath through a field, and is surrounded by trees.

SUNHONEY STONE CIRCLE

1. High Priest and Priestess Stones

This was the altarpiece of the old ceremonies, and much healing went on here, and many initiations into the realms of ancient lore took place. It is a unique balance of male and female energies. Sometimes it can be induced, but to place stones on groups of springs was common, and this site has uniqueness because the spring water spirals underneath this site, and there was once a well here, which wasn't present at every site.

The High Priest Stone on the left side looks like a Mayan or oriental ancient profile of a priest with a half-open shamanic eye. Within the energy force that surrounds this stone, there are seven chakra points with open eyes, representing them with a flash of sunlight at their centres, and radiate energy up and down the line of the eyes, and this energy comes down from the apex, and does enter the ground as well as the stone itself. This energy brings the fire of the solar energy of the sun, and also the power of stellar energy, since they are suns too. This reflects the wisdom that comes from farsighted 5th dimensional realms, like Sirius who inspired highly sophisticated cultures on Earth.

The High Priestess Stone on the right side also has a series of eye shapes beside it, representing the chakra system, and inside the 'iris' of the eyes, there are chalices, for the energy comes straight from the Earth, and rises to the apex above the stone. Out of the top of the stone there is a bulbous mass of energy with energy going upwards and downwards, above and below this, and inside the energy there is another eye with a chalice in the iris, and it is the seventh eye in the group. So the Priest Stone brings energy down from Heaven to Earth, and the High Priestess Stone brings energy up from Earth to Heaven.

In the centre between the two stones is the Feminine Energy Stone, which has cup and ring markings on it, and it is a recumbent stone. Out of this stone a very large, slowly spiralling energy emanates from the Earth, rising majestically, and it is the place where the strongly spiralling springs are situated.

This differs from the High Priestess Stone, because this is purely the energy of the Earth left as it is, whereas, the High Priestess Stone is very much drawing on the stone of the planet, in which is held many memories of other high priestesses who have never been on this planet, so much spirit memory comes up here, and can be seen in this way at many other sites of the same kind.

Another recumbent stone lies upon the ground in front of the altar at a perpendicular angle to the Feminine Stone, and it has a large, high, arched flame energy emanating from it. It is a link to the light at the centre of the Earth, because a high priest or priestess was aware of Ashanti, the place where advanced people live inside the earth, and could link to the domain and share wisdom here when the stone was upright.

This is because the wisdom complemented the Altar Stones, and is strangely profound, for this was the element of fire seen here, water from the spring at the Feminine Energy Stone, earth and water at the High Priestess Stone, and air and fire at the Priest Stone, and so the Feminine Energy Stone is very well- balanced.

Male Priest Stone message:
"I am a long standing stone, giving fatherly energies to the site. I offered much at the time of use, and many came to pluck wisdom of Heaven and Earth to give to others. I was overlit by beings from higher worlds, who channelled information through to the priests, who in turn, gave to the people. Sometimes lay people were allowed in en masse, into the centre of the circle, flanked by priests and priestesses."

Priestess Stone message:
"May the Goddess be with you, our blessings to all who come here. Our love of God and Goddess gave this place a sanctity in times past, and some of that remains. All who tune in and ask for light, enhances. The central Feminine Energy Stone was upright once, and links male and female energies."

SUNHONEY STONE CIRCLE

2. Initiation of Secrets Stone

"I was the stone that helped people choose which stone to stand by, according to their status or character.

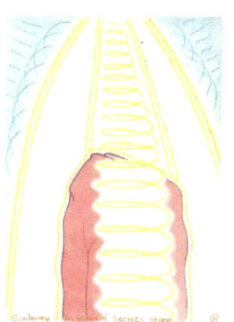

Each person in turn would come to me in order to seek something they needed to search for within, and this would be enhanced by tuning into me."

This stone is for a Priestess and a creative person. This type of stone exists at other sites and circles, so seek it out, for there is always an Initiator of Secrets Stone, for healing and creativity, and I offer it in my unique way."

Energy comes up from the Earth in a slow gentle spiral, to meet energy coming downwards from heavenly spheres, to form a balanced energy, and its epicentre is above the stone, and it resonates with the crown chakra.

The energy I felt was stimulating my feet and the energy over my head, thus Heaven and Earth, and in initiating secrets, they are illuminating, but different for each person.

I saw a cobra's head over the top of the stone bobbing up and down, which is also a good sign, and indicative of spiritual wholeness.

SUNHONEY STONE CIRCLE

3. Thought Edifier Stone

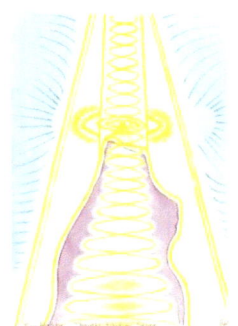

"I expand the intellect in the highest manner for those who need it. If there was a problem, people could gather round this stone to find a solution, and the energy here would help in that purpose."

There is brilliant light seen at the top of the stone, where there is an eye amidst the rapid spiralling motion that is coursing through the stone.

It begins broader at the base of the stone, gradually narrowing towards the top, and then remains constant. It continues up to the apex, which is where a downward directed shaft of light splays out from above, shining over the whole stone.

This spiralling energy strongly emanates from the Earth, and is suffused with the emerald green light, especially near and around the base, which slowly resonates its energy upwards to the rest of the stone.

At the apex, where the eye is, I see it suffused in brilliant white light, and it radiates energy outwards, stimulating the crown chakra and the mind to be alert and ready for inspiration that may pour in on that shaft of light stream that radiates from the eye.

It works for the higher mind, not the intellect, although the latter may be stimulated and inspired as a result, and the energy comes from the stars as well.

SUNHONEY STONE CIRCLE

4. Emotional Release Stone

"I am in touch with Earth energies a little more than some of the other stones, allowing gentle feminine energies to come and bathe people's spirits.

It is good for bereavements and difficult situations of any kind, for the energy, though strong, is gentle, and not as vibrant as the Thought Edifier Stone."

This is yet another spiral energy stone, and is broader at the base of the stone. The spirals stop at the apex, where there hovers a lotus flower energy, with sixteen petals around the edge, and three larger petals raised vertically in the centre. Out of the centre emanates another smaller spiral with radiant light streaming upwards.

Around the whole lotus and spirals area etc., there is a bowl shaped area of light encapsulating it, and the sides of it rise upwards to the same height as the stone below it, and within the base of the bowl shape there are forms that are petal-like edges and are small and look like a frilled edge.

The spiralling energy from the lotus rises to the top of the bowl shape, and the streaming energy or light is also radiating downwards too, which makes the lotus flower glow brightly.

The idea is to visualise yourself inside this bowl of light energy, and with the lotus flower, feeling the spiralling energy resonating through you. This energy resonates with the throat and emotional centres, related to the throat, or pockets and places where emotion is held in the body, and this bowl of energy helps to release it gently and gradually.

SUNHONEY STONE CIRCLE

5. The Tender Stone

"I have lots of gentle loving energy emanating from all angles to give the sensitive people more confidence. It is also for those who have lost their mothers, sisters or anyone close, and they need much support.

I finally bring out the emotions and emotionally charged thoughts, which individuals hold in their guts, hearts and mind, and help it all to go."

At the centre of the stone is a shining heart, radiating light on all sides, 360 degrees. Above the stone, half the height of the stone again, hangs an 'eye' energy. This emanates a gently rippling shaft of light down over the heart energy, to the base of the stone, and the width of the shaft widens as it descends, until it stretches to encapsulate the base of the stone.

Another shaft of light which is the full width of the stone projects light from heavenly places too, and is straight and vertical sided. Also, a beam of light comes from the eye and stretches over to this vertical shaft, which projects light into the heart to maintain its energy level.

This rippling shaft is the tender energy that gently waves over a person, and resonates with their heart to lift its state to one nearer to being peaceful.

The straight-sided shaft is pure energy coming from spirit, and it also strengthens both of the shafts coming from the eye.

The other shaft that links the eye to the vertical shaft also links the eye of the Source energy to that of the immediate, from the higher planes.

It is a very feminine energy where there is no judgement, only universal compassion.

SUNHONEY STONE CIRCLE

6. The Garland Stone

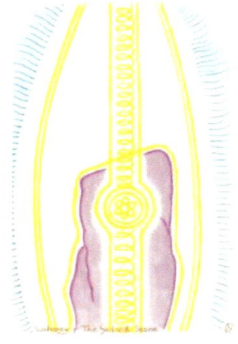

"The person here is given honour and grace, and is the first to receive blessings from the Altar Stone, i.e. the Priest or Priestess. It was important to have one of each gender.

The balance of male and female energies is also there in my midst, because I link Heaven and Earth energies via my column of light, which is drawn to a central point near the top of me, where a circular sphere of light holds the energy of the solar power, shown by the three ovals that intersect each other, and are always in motion like a gyroscope.

The central column holds spiral energy that comes from the Earth, and the convex shaft of light that encompasses the whole of the column and the stone is of the Heavens.

It is the sun image at the centre that makes the shaft of light convex, and could it represent the Central Spiritual Sun too?

The energy is radiated outwards, not stridently but gently, and at certain times of the year, the perimeter of the shaft of light has a thick outline that effervesces and undulates within itself, and so to an onlooker, it looks like a garland, and would be offered to a neophyte about to be initiated, or someone who deserved an extra blessing.

SUNHONEY STONE CIRCLE

7. The Opener of the Third Eye Stone

"I enhance people's third eyes so they can gain inner wisdom by the usual sending of energy up the spine via the two channels, Ida and Pingala, around to the third eye.

The neophyte's training for priesthood would draw them here; to discern their own inner state especially, to help them develop, for the journey truly starts with yourself, for with that clear vision, much is possible.

At the apex of the stone, there is a four-pointed star, with concentric layers, and at its centre is another image of the triple ovals that gyrate around each other, denoting sun-like energies, but with the stellar shape around it, the image may refer to another star out in space.

There is a shaft of light coming down through the stone, and it emanates from a ring of fiery light well above the apex and the four-pointed star.

The shaft widens as it comes downwards, but its width is still well within the diameter of the stone, and it holds a spiralling energy, for the shaft comes downwards to meet the earth, and draws the spiralling energy that comes up through the shaft of light.

There is also another shaft of light that is very wide, and encompasses the area well beyond the stone, but is narrow at the top as it emanates from the ring of fiery light, which looks like an eye from this angle.

It is the third eye in fact, and also the eye of the Source, and this Source can bring great clarity, and as it can draw up Earth energy strongly, it will have that dorje or thunderbolt energy of sudden illumination within its capacity.

SUNHONEY STONE CIRCLE

8. The Warrior Stone

"I give much energy for courage to people. The energy that comes to me, I flow it through people straight to their hearts, and all people can really benefit from it."

In the image, a column of light comes down through the centre of the stone, it is parallel sided and encompasses just over half the width of the stone, and it is white light.

Just over the apex of the stone hangs a bright eye-shaped energy, which is as wide as the column of light. It has an image of a heart at the centre, within which is held a diamond. This means that the eye brings energy from the Source that is spiritual, for the heart, and will manifest in a more practical way for a person, where quick decisions are required.

The symbolism of the diamond is that it is the energy from spirit, i.e. the circle or disk, that has been earthed to a square formation, by taking on the four corners or elements, in order to manifest.

From that eye, four shafts of light radiate outwards in an St Andrew's Cross formation, except that in this case the arms are equidistant. These shafts add a force of energy to the image, giving it potency, which stridently flow through the aura radiantly to protect it.

SUNHONEY STONE CIRCLE

9. The Sword in the Stone

"I am the Excalibur stone and this is the wisdom that is immersed in nature, and it is for the wise ones who can extract it, they shall be the Excalibur holders! I have a blissful energy that lifts the soul.

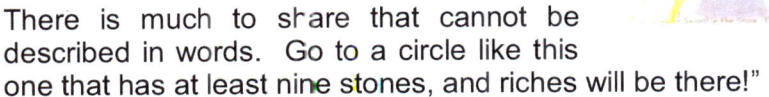

There is much to share that cannot be described in words. Go to a circle like this one that has at least nine stones, and riches will be there!"

The stone is barely visible at the subtle level due to its energies being so powerful. It is a tall stone with a pointed top, and at its apex is a huge eye with a four-pointed star inside, and it hovers like an interstellar Mother spaceship.

Inside the four-pointed star is a spiralling energy that is like the centre of the Source, and the Mother aspect of it. Out of the eye, four huge shafts of white light radiate in the St Andrew's Cross formation, as mentioned in the Warrior Stone, and these ones have a strongly dazzling energy.

In the crown, the energy unifies one with spirit,
In the third eye you become the 'knower' of all wisdom,
At the throat the vortex energy brings purification for greater communication with spirit,
In the heart there is a radiant blessing,
In the solar plexus the mind grows wise,
At the sacral there is a depth of compassion and creative initiative to serve,
In the base chakra there is the depth of unity with life in the here and now.

This is where the new initiate can learn to develop his or her wisdom.

SUNHONEY STONE CIRCLE

10. The Releasing Stone

"I am called the Releasing Stone because I am able to be a catalyst to let the energies of emotional and mental issues go, from within the group and circle collectively, for those who come here for solace, either singly or as a group, whether they hold a ceremony or not.

As I am the ninth stone, this is to be expected! I bring in energy from Heaven and Earth, and transmute all I come across, God bless."

Many circles were built with a determined number of stones, and nine was a common number used, with their title being 'nine stones', such as the one at Winterbourne Abbas, another near Matlock in Derbyshire, and also one near St Just in Cornwall, to name a few.

There is a huge shaft of light that envelopes the stone, and comes from an 'unseen' destination, but there is the indication that it comes from Source, or the Great Mystery, as there is a radiant diamond with a swirling energy within it.

The major component in this image is the huge energy force that hangs over the stone. It is a disk of light that also surrounds the light shaft, and at its centre is a mass of tubes seen end-on.

They are called spirillae, and they draw off unwanted energy with remarkable efficiency, so all that is released can be instantly drawn up and away.

The shaft also produces light, which will enhance this happening. Healing as in a deep peace is what remains, after this structure has worked, and that energy is felt in this stone.

SACRED SITES & PLACES OF POWER
THE SCOTTISH ORACLE CARDS
Element - Ether

INSIGHTS OF THE SUNHONEY STONE CIRCLE

This set deals with final release of individual karmic connections, so the individual can focus on higher frequencies available via this set. It also links to higher frequency energy in the Earth, and can be directed as needed.

1. <u>The Initiation of Secrets Stone</u>. There is a deep archaic and timeless link to the Mother Gaia and Goddess energy here. I saw a dark cave-like entrance for a while. It is like this card, and links to the core of life on Earth. I could feel white energy oozing out of the Earth with this card, and permeating everywhere.
2. <u>The Thought Edifier Stone</u>. 'Through my spiralling energy, and the radiant third eye, I send pulses of energy to permeate the individual's mind, so he or she can bring in good energy. The mind is aided, as this energy permeates the mind to bring peace, and like being given a healing, all concerns seem insignificant, and they fade away, and more of spiritual interest will come in.' Try again for more wisdom, next time.
3. <u>The Emotional Release Stone</u>. I felt a gentle sense of everything being taken by the stone's energy, and drawn up into the light, from the sacral, heart and in the head. I don't have a lot of emotional past life stuff around me, as I used to do, though there may be pockets still, but they will be small, since my inner peace is growing each day.
4. <u>The Tender Stone</u>. It links head and heart energies in its actions, but the emphasis is on the heart. The energy endeavours to help a person to love themselves to the degree the Divine Mother loves us.
5. <u>The Garland Stone</u>. This holds the deep peace of nature, like a summer's day, of abundant wildflowers. It also consolidates the energies of Heaven and Earth, bringing them to a focal point at the heart, and encircling the heart with this energy of nature, hence the garland stone. I could feel this energy gently settling around the heart, creating a sense of unity.

6. <u>The Opening of the Third Eye Stone</u>. The energy of the Garland Stone is taken higher to the Third Eye, in this instance. The Third Eye is focused on, and the star-like energy helps to dissipate any lower energies of the personality that may impede the concentration, or help those energies to be reconciled, as appropriate.
7. <u>The Warrior Stone</u>. The energy of this stone makes the individual very focused and single minded, in his or her purpose in life. Hence the term, and is ideal for a warrior to use before any challenging battles and other difficult moments. I have seen this energy format at two sites, where one stone is called the Warrior Stone, and the other is nearby and is linked to it. Of course, we have inner 'battle sites', which need focusing on to bring to peaceful conclusions.
8. <u>The Sword in the Stone</u>. A good, strong and peaceful card! This card shows the culmination of the Garland Stone into the third eye, linked to the Warrior Stone, so there is a consolidation of heart and third eye energy, leaving the lower mind behind, to link with the Divine. The Sword in the Stone signifies for me, the link of male energy with the stone of the Earth Mother, female energy, to create unity. To be an Excalibur remover from the stone would mean knowing how to transform energy and use it, but in this case, it is best united with the feminine energy. I could feel the energy of deep bliss beginning to fill my whole being.
9. <u>The Releasing Stone</u>. I feel this stone releases a person from the energy field of the Earth, or aims to! Within the diamond at the apex of the stone, there is a spiralling energy that galvanises itself as a catalyst. It generates much energy as a result, which filters through the spirillae below it in abundance, bathing the individual in a stream of dynamic energy.
10. <u>The Priest & Priestess Stones Altarpiece</u>. If you knelt here by these stones and meditated, you would soon find yourself linking with the spirits who used this circle, and they would instruct you in whichever way you wish. From a particular time period, the name of the priestess is Alythia, and the priest is Harydwyn. They spent long hours meditating and doing ceremonies here. The people in the community they served would come to ask questions, ask for healing on behalf of themselves and others. They would give the healing on site ideally, since the energy was so good, but go

to people if they couldn't get to the stones. The energy here is very high frequency and is the highest of all the stones, and it has a feeling of surrounding the individual in a strong ball of energy, and I could see a bright light within the centre of this structure.

The cards were repeated again

1. The Initiation of Secrets Stone – The casting off of old clothes, old ways of being, old habits and outworn attitudes will bring in new treasures and riches. A flooding in of spiritual light can then come in, which protects and inspires constantly, and lifts you to blissful states.
2. The Thought Edifier Stone – This ensures that unwanted thoughts are transmuted, and that the ego begins to link with the Divine, and melds into a unified state.
3. The Emotional Release Stone – Holding this card at the third eye will help remove any old memories from past lives that the ego is holding onto, and it brings out the emotion held in the respective parts of the body, and I found it comforting, because the card holds the energy of the stone itself, and hence, there is a link with its presence, and associated spirits overlighting. I had an old memory that the card helped to shift.
4. The Tender Stone – Having a heart in the centre of this image, a flood of white energy came in from above, as per the image, and a burst of loving energy radiated through me.
5. The Garland Stone – I felt a sense of disunity, and once it was pinpointed, the Garland Stone resumed its aura of unified state around me, and so it helped to highlight the problem, which was resolved. It can create its unified state within each chakra, to help focus on where any given problem is coming from.
6. The Opening of the Third Eye Stone – In opening the third eye, it strengthens this area, for it will be opening it further than it was before, 'in order to reach more Godwards. Ask that it only opens as much as you can manage to deal with at that moment in time.' I could feel more light and good energy coming in, and saw a very calm pond mirroring the surrounding foliage. It is likened to the soul mirroring the Divine, and when the ego has gone into the background, to cause fewer disruptions.

7. The Warrior Stone – That consolidation of energy that the Warrior Stone has, enhances the third eye area, as previously worked on. It holds a grail like mien to it, like the next card does, that timeless search for the unity with the Divine Source, and in this case, via the consolidation at the Third Eye in a single-minded way. It is the spiritual warrior.
8. The Sword in the Stone – I focused for a while, and the image revealed that fiery energy that was waiting to ignite. For it holds Heaven and Earth in unity, and when the focus is right, it will bring to the fore, a blazing light that radiates from within your soul.
9. The Releasing Stone – When a whole mass of light came through via the spirillae structures in the image, I then realised that the stone is geared to releasing light, as well as to helping a person release energy and traits not needed any more. Also, to release from karmic debts. Do ask for your own guidance on this matter, as with all the other cards.
10. The Priest and Priestess Stones Altarpiece – Alythia and Harydwyn welcomed me to the altar, and said that they would ask me into a ceremony at their site the next time I meditated. They invited me to imbibe of the energy on site at the altarpiece for now, and I'm still buzzing with the energy as I write. They may ask you to do the same.

I saw Alythia the High Priestess in the centre of the circle, and she asked me to choose which stone I wished to stand beside, while experiencing the ceremony. I visualised the site, and ended up at the stone to the right side of the Altar Stones, as looking from within, with my back to the stones. This was the Releasing Stone, which Alythia said was very appropriate. Just then I was whisked out of the circle, due to some clearing that was required, and couldn't be inside the circle until it was completed, as my energy was too low. I still found myself bobbling around like a balloon in the wind, always due to instability of the subtle bodies, once cleared, cleansed, at peace and settled down, then it stabilises.

Once inside again, she handed me a light, and said to give it to the Earth, not in the circle, but where I am at, at home at that moment. She gave a run down of the ceremony at the basic level, casting the circle; everyone else who was present was to be gathered at the stones of their choice, who I was aware of to a degree later on, the ceremony, sending out of the light. At the next level, she gave each of us a seed thought to consider. Happily no one knew what the other's seed thought was. Mine was 'assurance', and I pondered its potential for me, for a while. Words like stability, strength, sure mindedness, etc, came to me, and no doubt it was an encouragement in my life at present, to be added to it, in order to add more lustre, sense of purpose, and to get me away from the 'sidelines' more so.

I had not seen Harydwyn as yet, and then Alythia went to the altar, and he was doing something there. What he was focusing on was an image representing myself. I couldn't see what it depicted as yet, but I was invited to take it home and place it somewhere safe until I could examine it later. I brought it through into my bedroom where I meditate, and placed it in the bedside table drawer. Harydwyn said that once I had figured out what it meant, then I could return to the circle.

A final note here, the energy of the circle was given out to us at the end of the ceremory, before the picture was given to me. With all that energy given to me, I rose into the air and then came down again. Alythia said that this latter experience meant that I wasn't quite ready yet to be fully buoyant.

Other words for 'assurance' of note are: terms of peace, a promise making a thing certain, engagement, pledge, guarantee, self-confidence, steadfastness, intrepidity, security, certainty and trust.

Alythia later asked me what the rising in the air meant. I half joked, and said a high priestess, while trying to think of what else it could mean. When I was unable to think of anything, she said it meant that I'd have an affinity with higher realms, on and off the planet.

I asked her about what would happen with the 2012 situation, and she advised that nature could tell me, and would also tell me what 'news' there was on the go, and it would be good, not bad. The method is to pick a stone or place best suited to the job, and keep linking in to ensure I'd get the relevant information, on a regular basis.

I checked out the image in the bedside table drawer, which turned out to be a necklace, and it came out of the image and I put it on. It consisted of clear quartz, amethyst, rose and rutile. It made me feel calm, more resolute, as per the 'assurance' given yesterday. I could feel it pulsing, and it also reminded me of a stone circle's energy.

There was some clearing to do, as usual, for the necklace elucidated my state of being 'in exile' or on hold, due to the power I had in past lives, and the karmic obligation to do humble things and inner work in this life so far, so that I could redress the balance, and then move forward with a fresh slate.

This is what the necklace is portraying for me, and also encouraging me to be self-assured now, as if to say, it is all right, the work is about done, and the exile is all but over! You can 'come out' once more! Very encouraging.

Having done that, the words 'you are now ready to return to the circle' came to me.

This was a session to ascertain any ties with people in my life. Alythia said that people pop up in my life, so that ties from the past can be cleared. In order to see if any further ties were to be done, she said to just look into the light in front of you, and ask for anyone to appear visually or verbally, after a while, there was 'no more'. No more emotional ties would be lovely. That concluded the session for a break time.
Alythia talked to me about the fact that I could very easily link to ancient sites, and if I wished to go to ones I haven't visited, just to ask the spirits to take me there.

She said that the Welsh book of the Sacred Sites Series would be a story line, portraying my involvement, as well as anecdotes etc., of the past times, showing wisdom and insights of Wales, an important storyline as yet untold.

As for Sunhoney Circle, Alythia and Harydwyn have been around for centuries, and it has been a sacred site long before the stones were placed there, as people would gather there, and ask for inspiration and wisdom. The area became energised, because it was a favourable site in the first instance, and focusing on bringing energy down, along with prayers, created a strong resonance over time.

I then saw Harydwyn holding a sword, and he asked me if I knew the meaning of a sword. I mentioned that, apart from protection, its power can cut through illusion, and is a symbol of power and strength.

He also added that everyone on the spiritual path, who links to Sunhoney Stone Circle, could be allowed to receive the blessings of this sword. Harydwyn then placed the sword upon each of my shoulders, and on the crown. I could feel the energy strengthening my system, as a result.

They said that not as many people came for blessings from them these days, so they hope that these cards will help to change that. Other people may receive completely different experiences there, compared to mine!

**The History
Sunhoney Stone Circle**

This is another of the recumbent stone circle group, and is 25.3 metres in diameter. There are nine upright stones, one recumbent and two flankers. The upper side of the recumbent stone has thirty-one cup marks on it. The recumbent stone is of grey granite and the upright stones are red granite. At the recumbent stone circles, the cup marks are always on the recumbent stones and the stones in their vicinity, usually the flankers, and in some cases the stones nearby to them.

There is a ring cairn inside the circle, in a central position. Each of the stones of the circle stood originally, and stood on small cairns.

A RESUMÉ OF THE SITES FOR QUICK REFERENCE

In the following pages there is a quick checklist of all the sites with the names of the individual stones within that circle, and their gifts they hold. This is so that you can obtain the basic theme that each stone holds for when you may wish to attune to them.

Here are the five circles and their respective elements

<u>12 Apostles Circle</u> – air element
<u>Mother Circle</u> –   water element
<u>Loanhead of Daviot Circle</u> – earth element
<u>Easter Arquoithies Circle</u> – fire element
<u>Sunhoney Circle</u> – ether element

THE TWELVE APOSTLES STONE CIRCLE
The element of air

1. <u>The God's Altar Stone</u> – a stabilising link to heaven and earth.
2. <u>The Governor Stone</u>- an anti surge suppressor, bringing earth energy via the outlier.
3. <u>The Harmoniser Stone</u> – an energy purifier.
4. <u>The Evening Star Stone</u> – a place of alignment and scrying.
5. <u>The Gatekeeper Stone</u> – a meditation stone and for insights.
6. <u>The Storekeeper Stone</u> – a place of strong energy, 'lights the fires of the mind'. Elevated Chair of the Druids.
7. <u>The Watch Stone</u> – a presider over ceremonies, a guardian stone.
8. <u>The Grail Cup Stone</u> – a place for teaching, transformation and illumination.
9. <u>The Knowledge Stone</u> – the lighter of the way.
10. <u>The Kind Stone</u> – a gentle reflective energy. Focuses on insights from the Gatekeeper Stone.
11. <u>The Druid Stone</u> – a place of Druidic wisdom, maturity and self-integration.

12. The Thunder Stone – brings in heavenly energy and from the central crystal. A kundalini stone.
13. The Outlier Stone – Constant energy source for the circle, the Thunder Stone's energy may be intermittent.

THE MOTHER STONE CIRCLE
The element of water

1. The Mother Stone – links to the Source, inspirer. Also like an outlier. The hub of the circle.
2. The Seer Stone – an earth link, and kundalini. Sees into past and present.
3. The Prophecy Stone – future information. Akashic record keeper.
4. The Ring Stone – the blessing place for couples to harmonise before marriage. All major decisions.
5. The Fairy Stones – bringer of green light from nature. A place of reflection and wisdom.
6. The Guides – the governor stones of this circle, the anti surge suppressor.
7. The Sacred Stones – a place of healing, from physical to soul levels.
8. The Altar Stones – the place where the high priestess placed good power objects and items for ceremonial use. Illumination.

THE LOANHEAD OF DAVIOT STONE CIRCLE
The element of earth

1. The Altar Stones – inspiration and enhancement of energy.
   High priest – energy from the heavens.
   High priestess – energy from the earth.

2. The Teaching Stone – inspiration and wisdom to teach others.
3. The Praying Stone – pray here to open the way forward in your life.
4. The Guider Stone – a guide to a solution for an appropriate course of action.
5. The Altar Reflector Stone – helps to deal with the subconscious.

6. The Dreamer Stone – the dreamtime, and higher mind and heart.
7. The Adoration Stone – a comforter, energy from the heavens for healing and inspiration.
8. The Mistletoe Stone – for ceremonial activities. A place of prayer and incantations.
9. The Ringleader Stone – this is like the Governor stones as at other circles.

EASTER ARQUOITHIES STONE CIRCLE
The element of fire

1. The Altar Stones
   High priest stone – for direction, strength and courage.
   High priestess stone – for earth energy, wisdom, healing and counselling.

2. The Scryer Stone – links to the Source for wisdom and illumination.
3. The Inspirer Stone – the Druid's 'Elevated Chair' of the east, dominion of the high priestess.
4. The Wisdom Stone – a purifier of energies for neophytes and individuals. Soul clearing preparation. Skill reclamation.
5. The Initiation Stone – energy renewal. Maturation and place of initiation.
6. The Saintly Stone – inspiration and strength for masterhood/high positions.
7. The Grounding Stone – the energies help you to give out energy, skills and wisdom.
8. The Effulgence Stone – promotes a clear-sighted knowingness and great strength.
9. The Sage Stone – aids insight into other states of being on more advanced worlds.
10. The Searcher Stone – a freer of energies to move where one wills. Cosmic life view.

THE SUNHONEY STONE CIRCLE
The element of ether

1. The Altar
   High Priest Stone – solar and stellar energy.

High priestess Stone – earth energies, Ashanti and energy spirals.

2. Initiation of Secrets Stone – healing and creativity. Helps people to search within.
3. Thought Edifier Stone – a problem solver and bringer of inspiration, enhances higher mind to work.
4. Emotional Release Stone – bereavements and other difficult situations. Releases.
5. The Tender Stone – a comforter and another place to release emotions. Warms the heart.
6. The Garland Stone – a balancer of male and female energies.
7. The Opener of the Third Eye Stone – sends kundalini energy to enhance the 3rd eye.
8. The Warrior Stone – for courage, a peaceful heart, also alert and quick-wittedness.
9. The Sword in the Stone – nature's wisdom. Bliss to uplift the soul. Self-development.
10. The Releasing Stone – a catalyst for release. Heaven & earth energies. Transmutation.

HEATHER'S WORK PHILOSOPHY

This describes my method of approach to my work, which began with paintings, and is now incorporated into my books.

Heather's work is generally based on meditations and dreams, and is her personal method of exploration into the nature of other realms through sensing and portraying the visual forms and energies in various places and states of being.

Her themes are based on nature in its various aspects, such as cloudscapes, inspiring mountains, movements of water, as well as sacred sites, stone circles and the planets of our solar system. She has also done paintings of many sacred sites and wells, homeopathic remedy images, and crystals, and is now exploring codes.

Her interest and concern is that the paintings are of a healing and inspiring nature, for she has always been just as interested in healing as she has in art. She would like to think that she is focusing harmony and healing through the paintings as an offering of service and pleasure to others.

When she goes to a sacred site she can see and feel the energy present like a shining presence coming through her, and she can also pick up this quality from a site through a photograph too.

Visionary painting for her is part of a soul searching, universal searching into realms of discovery within the portals of God's creation, echoing the energies seen in meditation or visions.

For on the physical level energies do not seem a reality for all is slow and little vibrancy is apparent. However, on other levels everything sparkles and vibrates like bright sunlight on water, or transforming fluid patterns, for all is in motion, singing and dancing, and that the universe dances like the Song Celestial.

CONTACT DETAILS

A new website is happening within the near future and will have my paintings and books, and also some of my mother's books.

Many of the books in my website are presently on Amazon, and others will be put on site periodically.

Books presently on Amazon:

Sacred Sites and Places of Power 1
A Meditational Handbook
Sacred Sites and Places of Power 2
Amaleina's Journey
Seeds of Amaranth 1 – Recovering the Caskets
Seeds of Amaranth 2 – Re-Activating the Codes
Seeds of Amaranth 3 – Resuming the Eternal Legacy
Channelled Teachings from Sananda & Master R (1-5) –
Beryl Charnley
Channelled Teachings from the Devic Kingdom (1-4) –
Beryl Charnley
Channelled Communications from Sirius, Arcturus,
Pleiades & Betelgeuse (1-4) – Beryl Charnley

Other items for sale:

The Atlantean Chakra Ki Cards – card set
Inspired by the trilogy and work on our chakras
Sacred Sites & Places of Power 3
The Scottish Oracle Cards – card set to go with this book

More books coming soon!

The website for books, art & oracle cards-
www.heathercharnleyspiritualart.co.uk

Heather can be contacted as given below for all enquiries
heathercharnley@googlemail.com
Books are being traded under **Purple Spirit Press**.
The email for the books and paintings is as above also on –

purplespiritpress@gmail.com

www.ingramcontent.com/pod-product-compliance
Lightning Source LLC
Chambersburg PA
CBHW042340150426
43196CB00001B/5